THE
PRINCIPAL
INFLUENCE

ASCD
ALEXANDRIA, VIRGINIA USA

THE PRINCIPAL INFLUENCE

A Framework for Developing Leadership Capacity in Principals

PETE
HALL

DEBORAH
CHILDS-BOWEN

ANN
CUNNINGHAM-MORRIS

PHYLLIS
PAJARDO

ALISA
SIMERAL

ASCD®

1703 N. Beauregard St. • Alexandria, VA 22311-1714 USA
Phone: 800-933-2723 or 703-578-9600 • Fax: 703-575-5400
Website: www.ascd.org • E-mail: member@ascd.org
Author guidelines: www.ascd.org/write

Deborah S. Delisle, *Executive Director*, Stefani Roth, *Publisher*; Genny Ostertag, *Director, Content Acquisitions*; Julie Houtz, *Director, Book Editing & Production*; Jamie Greene, *Editor*; Melissa Johnston, *Graphic Designer*; Mike Kalyan, *Manager, Production Services*; Keith Demmons, *Production Designer*; Andrea Wilson, *Senior Production Specialist*

PAPERBACK ISBN: 978-1-4166-2144-7   ASCD product #116026   n1/16
PDF E-BOOK ISBN: 978-1-4166- 2145-4; see Books in Print for other formats.

Quantity discounts: 10–49, 10%; 50+, 15%; 1,000+, special discounts (e-mail programteam@ascd.org or call 800-933-2723, ext. 5773, or 703-575-5773). For desk copies, go to www.ascd.org/deskcopy.

Library of Congress Cataloging-in-Publication Data

Names: Hall, Peter A., 1971- author.
Title: The principal influence : a framework for developing leadership
  capacity in principals / by Pete Hall, Deborah Childs-Bowen, Ann
  Cunningham-Morris, Phyllis Pajardo, Alisa A. Simeral.
Description: Alexandria, VA : ASCD, [2016] | Includes bibliographical
  references and index.
Identifiers: LCCN 2015040015 | ISBN 9781416621447 (pbk.)
Subjects: LCSH: School principals--United States. | Educational
  leadership--United States. | School management and organization--United
  States.
Classification: LCC LB2831.92 .H35 2016 | DDC 371.2--dc23 LC record available at http://lccn.loc.
gov/2015040015

25 24 23 22 21 20 19 18 17 16   2 3 4 5 6 7 8 9 10 11 12

THE PRINCIPAL INFLUENCE

Acknowledgments

To say this book was a collaborative effort would really be a seismic understatement. And that's not just to recognize the fact that we had five authors dedicated to the project, researching, drafting, editing, revising, and wrestling with one another for several months in an attempt to get it right. Rather, the product that you hold in your hands (or are scrolling through on your tablet) is the result of a compilation of the research, experience, expertise, and efforts of the many conscientious educators across the globe whose work we've leaned upon. Truly, this book sits on the shoulders of giants.

First, we owe a debt of gratitude to the past and present ASCD leaders and dozens of practitioners who created, refined, and shared the original ASCD Leadership Development Framework (which you'll read about shortly). Their work and vision set the foundation that we've built upon here. To the many authors, researchers, teachers, and leaders whose work we've shared—imitation is the sincerest form of flattery, right?—we offer another giant *thank you*. Many of the tools, strategies, and ideas you'll encounter in this book are the product of the great minds and successful practices of those who rolled up their sleeves before us, and some are only slightly modified from their original versions to meet our needs here.

To the good people at ASCD who shared a vision with us and entrusted us to carry out that vision with pertinacity and vigor, we provide this text as a symbolic gesture of our appreciation. This is a project that we hope carries the voices of educators past and present, inspiring the actions of the educators of today and tomorrow. Leadership matters, and it is our uniform and unyielding belief that by strengthening the leadership corps, we will positively impact the profession and our student learning outcomes. This is ASCD's vision, and we hope to have brought it to life in the pages that follow.

Lastly, we thank each and every one of you. If you are reading this, that indicates you have established a commitment to carrying out this vision. You have prioritized leadership for learning. You have formalized your passion, your calling, your mission. For our children and for our future, we thank you.

PART I

Why Leadership?

Leadership. Entering that simple keyword into any Internet search engine will return millions of hits in a fraction of a second. Further investigation of these sources will confirm what you already knew: leadership is a complex, subtle, delicate, and dynamic concept. In our schools, districts, and education systems, we must have leaders—effective leaders—to achieve the results that our society requires. As Stronge, Richard, and Catano state, "One essential ingredient for success in education and any business, for that matter, is effective leadership" (2008, p. xii).

Any discussion of leadership in education includes a nod to the building leader: the school principal. In a role that encapsulates the varied and nuanced work of middle management—and extends beyond plant maintenance and compliance to include counseling, budgeting, inspiring, teaching, learning, disciplining, evaluating, buffering, celebrating, consoling, and a million other tasks—the principal is indeed the CLO (Chief Learning Officer). Ultimately, student performance expectations rest squarely on the shoulders of the principal.

Quite simply, the school principal is arguably the most influential position in education today. This statement does not diminish the impact of district superintendents, state department officials, legislators, the U.S. secretary of education, and the legions of professional teachers and educators improving children's lives on a daily basis; rather, it acknowledges the unique positional influence held by the building administrator. Who else but the principal builds a more substantial bridge between policy and practice?

Kenneth Leithwood and his colleagues found that "it turns out that leadership not only matters; it is second only to teaching among school-related factors in its impact on student learning" (2004, p. 3). Principals, in particular, must create both a school culture and infrastructure that support effective teaching and learning practices by transforming the structures, processes, and performance throughout the school environment (Childs-Bowen, Moller, & Scrivner, 2000).

In John Hattie's meta-analysis of the factors that influence student achievement (2009), 27 of the top 30 (ranked by effect size) are school-, teacher-, and curriculum-based, all of which are directly influenced by the building principal. Furthermore, über-researcher Bob Marzano notes that leadership could well be considered "the single most important aspect of effective school reform" (2003, p. 172). In a summation we welcome fondly, noted school leadership expert Douglas Reeves states quite plainly that "leadership matters" (2009, p. 107).

A Call for Sustainability

The demands on the principal in the Era of Accountability are as extensive and formidable as ever. It is well documented that the curious blend of increased public demand for results and the across-the-board disinvestment in education have resulted in a principalship that is defined by stress, moving targets, heightened responsibility, and a remarkable turnover rate. Unfortunately, it's no surprise that a recent report indicates that over one-fifth of new principals leave the job within two years (Burkhauser, Gates, Hamilton, & Ikemoto, 2012).

Alarmingly, the WestEd Center for the Future of Teaching and Learning reports that principals are dealing with competing pressures that may ultimately make the job untenable (Bland et al., 2011). It would appear that we're tugging at the rope from both ends: effective principal leadership is critical to school success, yet the job itself is virtually impossible to accomplish. Frequent turnover, daunting challenges, overwhelming responsibilities, and stressed-out principals just aren't good for kids, teachers, districts, or the future of our society. The time is now to attend to the ongoing growth, support, and development of our school principals.

Building Leadership Capacity

"If we are to succeed as an educational enterprise in a highly competitive world, then we must embrace leadership development—not in a cursory fashion, but rather in an ongoing, comprehensive, sustained manner" (Stronge et al., 2008, p. xii). And if the principal is such an important driver in the educational engine, then it would behoove us as educators to embrace a comprehensive and detailed description of effective leadership approaches. To that end, because of its rich history of taking effective leadership research and making it practical for use in schools and districts, ASCD composed the first iteration of its Leadership Development Framework in 2008.

Based on existing and emerging research on effective school leadership and aligned with the 2008 Interstate School Leadership Licensure Consortium (ISLLC) Standards (with a definitive bent toward *instructional* leadership), the original ASCD Leadership Development Framework provided guidelines for what successful principals do. Created, vetted, and refined over an 18-month period by internal ASCD leaders and an external team of school and district leaders, state department of education leaders, and ASCD Faculty members with leadership development expertise, this document provided a suitable frame for expressing the core characteristics of effective instructional leadership.

As the role of the principal has evolved over the years, and as the ISLLC standards and other leadership standards were revisited and revised, ASCD was inspired to update its work, now titling it the *Principal* Leadership Development Framework, to better address a handful of key questions.

What does effective school-based instructional leadership look like? ASCD's Principal Leadership Development Framework (or PLDF) establishes a clear and concise picture of effective building leadership, expressing the knowledge, skills, dispositions, and actions necessary for success as a principal. In essence, it provides a clear target to support the ongoing growth and development of our leaders.

In what ways is the Framework unique? Over the past seven decades, ASCD has built a brand and reputation on leading the discussion of research-based best practices in education by investigating, researching, proposing, and clarifying the characteristics, behaviors, attitudes, and approaches of effective school leaders. A scan of the PLDF will reveal a significant tilt toward instructional leadership—as opposed to the duties of school management.

How does the Framework support principals' growth? There are two distinct pathways to access and utilize this tool: at the school level and at the district level.

- With a clear target in view, principals, assistant principals, and aspiring principals can address their own professional development needs. This is Pathway One, in which individual leaders create plans and execute them to bolster the practices, structures, and processes essential for sustained professional growth.
- In addition, the content and descriptions in the Framework can be integrated into the design of a sustainable district leadership development and coaching program for principals, assistant principals, and aspiring principals. Pathway Two, then, addresses the support provided to building leaders by their supervisors or other district-level leadership support networks.

Both of these pathways are explained in greater detail in Chapter 1.

What is the philosophy that drives the Framework? The ASCD PLDF is grounded in the belief that the growth of individual leaders and leadership teams leads to schoolwide and systemic growth that positively influences student learning. Just as we must build teachers' capacity to support ongoing growth and effectiveness in the classroom, so must we build leaders' capacity through continuous learning and reflective practice. This alignment provides a solid stanchion to which all of our approaches are inextricably connected.

How does reflective practice fit in the Framework? Having a list of effective leadership behaviors provides a clear target—a necessary, yet not sufficient, condition. Accurate, thorough, and continuous reflection will tip the balance. Effective leaders must be aware of their contextual reality, act with intentionality, assess the effect of their actions, and adjust course as necessary. In Chapter 2, we blend the

PLDF with the Principal's Continuum of Self-Reflection and the Reflective Cycle (Hall & Simeral, 2008, 2015), a potent combination of tools that help practitioners identify and strengthen their reflective habits. You'll notice the explicit inclusion of reflective practices woven throughout this text—indeed, self-reflection is the so-called red thread that connects our beliefs to our actions and will ultimately guide us to leadership success.

Leadership That Lasts

In any school environment, leadership is vital. Developing effective school leaders is a monumental responsibility, shared equally between the leaders themselves and their district counterparts.

From the demystification of effective leadership behaviors to the clarification of individual leadership strengths and collective systemic needs, school district officials and building administrators collaborating about continuous growth can have an immense effect on the ultimate results: increased student achievement. Using the ASCD PLDF, coupled with the Continuum of Self-Reflection and the Reflective Cycle, is an ideal strategy for acquiring that yield.

Complementary to any educator effectiveness model, principal evaluation model, or leadership rubric already in place in a district, this growth-oriented approach supports goal setting, planning, and strategic development of ongoing professional growth. Its reliance on building self-reflective abilities ensures an enduring, capacity-building impact on system, school, and individual leadership influences.

CHAPTER 1
The Principal Leadership Development Framework

There are many theories and approaches concerning the particular skills and strategies of effective leadership, and attempting to cover each component would prove cumbersome, exhausting, and fruitless. Instead, built upon the foundation provided by prominent researchers, educational thinkers, and practitioners, the ASCD Principal Leadership Development Framework (PLDF) emphasizes four key roles of the building administrator that are tied directly to instructional leadership:

- Principal as Visionary
- Principal as Instructional Leader
- Principal as Engager
- Principal as Learner and Collaborator

Further, the PLDF offers 17 criteria of effective practice that focus on the leadership behaviors with the greatest direct effect on the culture and status of learning and teaching within a particular school community (Figure 1.1).

Each of these roles and criteria will be described in further detail in Chapters 3–6. In the meantime, we want to make a couple of things clear: this is not an exhaustive list of the roles and responsibilities of the school principal. Since the job is so complex, that would prove unwieldy. In addition, this is not meant for principal evaluations. It is intended to provide clear targets to support the ongoing growth and development of our leaders. Effective use and application of the Framework will ensure that current and future building leaders—and those who support them—have a thorough and accurate picture of the actions that are tied most closely to instructional leadership.

Who Will Benefit from the Framework?

In a word: leaders (both site-based and district-level). Though we use the word *principal* almost exclusively throughout this book, the roles, approaches, and strategies are universal for various leaders at the school level, including assistant principals, aspiring principals, department chairs, teacher leaders, members of site leadership teams, and any other de facto leadership role at the building level. In addition, the

FIGURE 1.1

ASCD's Principal Leadership Development Framework

PRINCIPAL AS VISIONARY

1. Articulates, communicates, and leads the collaborative implementation and ongoing revision of the school's mission and vision.
2. Aligns and bases all decisions, practices, policies, and resources (e.g., human capital, time, budget, and facilities) on the school's mission and vision.
3. Promotes the collaborative creation, monitoring, and refinement of short- and long-term school improvement plans.
4. Compels the district and school community to embrace and work toward the attainment of the shared mission and vision.

PRINCIPAL AS INSTRUCTIONAL LEADER

1. Builds collective capacity of the entire staff through the cultivation of a robust Professional Learning Community.
2. Builds individual capacity of the entire staff through differentiated supervision, coaching, feedback, and evaluation practices.
3. Ensures the alignment of rigorous curricula, research-based best practices in instruction, and comprehensive formative and summative assessment approaches.
4. Promotes monitoring systems that use real-time data to inform instruction and intervention at the teacher, team, and school site levels.

PRINCIPAL AS ENGAGER

1. Maintains an unwavering priority of establishing and fostering an environment that tends to the whole child: healthy, safe, engaged, supported, and challenged.
2. Creates and cultivates partnerships within the parent, district, business, political, and greater community spheres to support the achievement of the school's mission and vision.
3. Drives and navigates positive change by assessing, analyzing, and anticipating emerging trends and implementing change-savvy techniques with staff and the school community.
4. Safeguards community values, ethics, and equitable practices, advocating for all children and displaying an appreciation for diversity.
5. Develops policies and practices that cultivate staff as reflective practitioners.

PRINCIPAL AS LEARNER AND COLLABORATOR

1. Facilitates the delivery of job-embedded, ongoing, coordinated professional learning opportunities that lead to increased student achievement.
2. Develops internal leaders and nurtures an environment of distributed leadership, collective responsibility, and collaborative decision making.
3. Models reflective practice, confidence, humility, perseverance, and interest in continuous growth and lifelong learning.
4. Participates regularly in professional learning organizations, a community of practice, and a leadership network.

Framework provides criteria and guidance for the district-level leadership roles—superintendents, school directors, assistant superintendents, principal supervisors, and others—who support the leadership development of current and future building-level leaders. District-level leaders, who may include curriculum coordinators and specialists, can also strengthen their instructional leadership practices by incorporating some of the strategies identified in this text into their regular professional practice.

Two Pathways to Build Leadership Capacity

There are two pathways for accessing and utilizing the PLDF, as mentioned in the Introduction:

- Pathway One: Individual leaders create plans and execute them to bolster the practices, structures, and processes essential for sustained professional growth.
- Pathway Two: The content and descriptions in the Framework can be integrated into the design of a sustainable district leadership development and coaching program for principals, assistant principals, and aspiring principals.

See Figure 1.2 for an illustration of these pathways, which are described in more detail in the sections that follow.

Pathway One: Individual Professional Growth

To create effective schools that have the strongest influence on student learning, development efforts must be embedded throughout all leadership roles, and professional learning experiences must be guided by a specific set of principles.

Growth and Development of Principals

Pursuing new learning, striving for continuous improvement, and building a never-ending repertoire of leadership skills are hallmark traits of effective school leaders (Marzano, Waters, & McNulty, 2005). Seated building principals—whether they are newly appointed, midcareer, or veteran educators—can all benefit from the identification and creation of key strategies, targeted goal setting, and deliberate job-embedded work plans to develop results from reflective leadership practices. Indeed, the school principal is at the heart of the Framework, hence its title: The *Principal* Leadership Development Framework. Principals can use this tool to take the reins of their own professional learning, boost their own reflective practice, and develop their own

FIGURE 1.2

Two Pathways for Accessing and Utilizing the ASCD Principal Leadership Development Framework

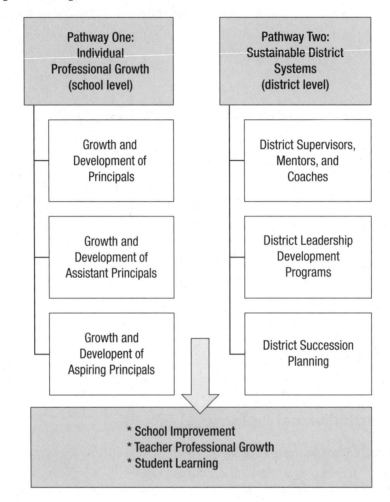

expertise. Thankfully, as Doug Reeves emphatically stated, "Excellent leadership is an acquired skill" (2002, p. 4).

Growth and Development of Assistant Principals

The position of assistant principal is one of the most dynamic, essential, and fluctuating roles in education, requiring a specific set of skills and dispositions (Pounder & Crow, 2005). At the same time, assistant principals are next in line to lead schools instructionally, yet they often assume the principalship unprepared to implement the practices of effective leadership. Traditionally, assistant principals serve as the chief disciplinarians, organize athletics, support the management of the building, lead extracurricular activities, and perform "other duties as assigned." In the Era of Accountability, those other duties must include instructional leadership. Assignments in leadership development programs for assistant principals and aspiring principals (and, to a lesser extent, teacher leaders) should mirror the work of a principal (Gallup, Inc., 2012). The PLDF provides direction and support for job-embedded leadership development activities to help individuals in these roles grow and transition.

Growth and Development of Aspiring Principals

Even before beginning down the path toward a principalship, aspiring administrators must have an accurate picture of what the position entails. The PLDF illustrates the necessary behaviors and approaches for effective leadership, which can help inform preservice administrators' intentional preparation strategies and direct district personnel as they "tap" candidates for leadership roles (Pounder & Crow, 2005). Aspiring principals tend to serve as de facto leaders within the building—in fact, it's been found that teacher leaders exert quite a bit of influence over their peers and other school leaders, illustrating the simultaneous top-down, bottom-up nature of change (Reeves, 2008). In this context, the PLDF also tends to the approaches that are intertwined with teacher leaders' daily routines and responsibilities, thereby cultivating leadership skills while in their current roles.

Pathway Two: Sustainable District Systems

The most popular definition of sustainability can be traced to a 1987 United Nations conference. In the 96th plenary meeting of the General Assembly, *sustainable developments* were defined as those that "meet present needs without compromising the ability of future generations to meet their own needs" (United Nations, 1987). Districts today are faced with the task of creating sustainable, renewable systems of leadership development that support future generations. With that in mind, the PLDF provides insights into the *what* and *how* of designing such systems.

District Supervisors, Mentors, and Coaches

School district officials have long felt the challenges associated with leading, motivating, and guiding the ongoing professional growth of building principals. The daunting question we pose is this: How do we lead the leaders? Embracing a philosophy of continuous improvement and assuming a growth mindset (Dweck, 2006), those in district leadership positions can indeed affect the thinking, decision making, planning, and actions of their seated principals. When professional development includes resources such as job-embedded coaching and feedback, educators are able to apply their new learning and skills at an increased rate of around 95 percent (Joyce & Showers, 1982). Within the PLDF are the tools for districts to tackle the ambitious and vital task of growing their leadership corps.

District Leadership Development Programs

From the district perspective, leadership development within the ranks is a top priority. Every member of the central or district office must understand effective leadership practices and act accordingly. The PLDF assists in the creation of dynamic and rigorous leadership development programs, inclusive of central office staff, that prepare the district to systematically tackle leadership capacity building that has a positive influence on student achievement. Indeed, "leadership is vital to the effectiveness of a school" (Marzano et al., 2005, p. 4). By extension, ensuring a robust pipeline of future positional leaders is vital to the effectiveness and survival of a district.

District Succession Planning

Twenty percent of first-year principals leave their schools within the first or second year, creating a domino effect that affects both teaching and student achievement (Burkhauser et al., 2012). Every school site within a district has particular needs, shaped in part by its unique demographics, climate, culture, and current contextual reality. Conducting a real-time needs assessment and matching principals' skills to particular assignments ensures that you can have the "right people in the right seats" at the right time (Collins, 2001, p. 41). Succession planning helps districts focus on leadership skill development and professional development opportunities (Hall, Salamone, & Standley, 2009). When a principal vacates a position, the district has an opportunity to maintain course or shift focus. It is the district's responsibility to ensure smooth, aligned, and thoughtfully planned transitions and a continued focus on successful progress during a change in leadership. Applying strategies from the PLDF can support such succession plans.

CHAPTER 2
Growing as Reflective Leaders

Benjamin Franklin once said, "Observe all men. Thyself most." It is with this in mind that we begin our journey toward understanding ourselves as leaders. For it's by knowing ourselves first that allows us to work with greater intentionality as we cultivate our leadership capacity. In John Dewey's words, "The self is not something ready-made but something in continuous formation through choice of action" (Dewey, 1933, p. 235). So how do we better understand ourselves as leaders within the Principal Leadership Development Framework? How do we grow in our capacity as visionaries? As instructional leaders? As engagers? As learners and collaborators? We use a tool called the Continuum of Self-Reflection.

The first iteration of the Continuum of Self-Reflection was detailed in *Building Teachers' Capacity for Success* (Hall & Simeral, 2008). Based on research that spans all the way back to Dewey's seminal *How We Think* (1910), Hall and Simeral describe four developmental stages through which teachers progress as they become skilled in the art of self-reflection: Unaware, Conscious, Action, and Refinement (see Figure 2.1). At its core, Hall and Simeral state, "the Continuum is a tool to help school leaders understand a teacher's current state of mind and identify the approaches that will encourage deeper reflective habits" (2008, p. 40).

FIGURE 2.1
Continuum of Self-Reflection

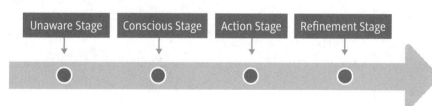

Subsequently, the principal's version of the Continuum of Self-Reflection, or P-CSR, was developed with descriptors distinct to the Principal Leadership Development Framework and for the purpose of helping school leaders—all school leaders—understand their current state of mind and assist in identifying specific behaviors that will foster more meaningful reflective habits.

As one might expect, the manner, depth, frequency, and accuracy with which a principal reflects on his or her professional experiences and responsibilities varies from individual to individual. As Figure 2.2 demonstrates, the Principal's Continuum of Self-Reflection is composed of the same four stages: Unaware, Conscious, Action, and Refinement. Although these stages are progressive, they are not categorical by definition. In fact, an individual may demonstrate characteristics of more than one stage simultaneously and be in different stages depending on the leadership criterion. The intent of the tool is to help leaders understand their current state of mind and identify the approaches that will encourage deeper reflective habits.

FIGURE 2.2

The Principal's Continuum of Self-Reflection

	UNAWARE STAGE	CONSCIOUS STAGE	ACTION STAGE	REFINEMENT STAGE
REFLECTIVE TENDENCIES	• Demonstrates little or no awareness of current reality in the school building and nuanced cultural context. • Oriented to routine. • Reacts emotionally or impulsively to the immediate needs of the school. • Focuses on the job itself—the tasks of the principalship.	• Demonstrates a consistent "knowing-doing" gap. • Offers explanations for problems and circumstances. • Misconstrues the factors requiring action. • Focuses first on self and one's own role in the principalship.	• Accepts responsibility for the success of students, staff, and self. • Evaluates situations objectively. • Seeks solutions to problems. • Focuses on the science of leadership, managing resources and implementing research-based practices.	• Recognizes there are multiple options to address every problem. • Maintains and seeks out a vast repertoire of leadership strategies. • Adjusts course when necessary to maintain heading toward common goal. • Focuses on the fluid art of leadership, seeking ongoing feedback and maintaining a relentless focus on continuous improvement.

The P-CSR in Action

To help understand the P-CSR and how a principal's thinking might affect his or her leadership behaviors, consider the following hypothetical example. See if you can recognize the descriptors within the P-CSR as we examine a leadership practice of our fictitious (but realistic) principal, Tim.

A couple of months into his eighth year as principal, Tim bumped into a respected colleague, Jade, at a district all-admin meeting. In their ensuing conversation, Jade mentioned that she'd been busy preparing for her upcoming monthly staff meeting. Surprised, Tim exclaimed, "Wow! How do you get away with monthly staff meetings? I thought all principals held them weekly. I can't go a week without touching base with my staff. There's just too much going on."

As Tim peppered her with questions, Jade shared that she works hard to respect teachers' time, opting to send a daily email to keep staff in the loop regarding upcoming events and business items, saving the significant communication for the monthly meeting. She explained that this frees up minutes—for her to foster the vision and for her teachers to collaborate—and ensures that their time together is focused and used wisely.

Tim was amazed at the idea. From the time he inherited the position from his predecessor seven years before, he had continued the routine of holding weekly staff meetings. That's just the way they've always done things at his school. He'd never taken the time to consider the impact or the possibility of changing that practice. For the sake of our story, he was firmly in the Unaware stage on the Continuum of Self-Reflection. He hadn't thought about or learned any different (and possibly more effective) ways of addressing the specific needs in his school other than what he'd already been doing.

"Give it a shot," Jade encouraged him. "Your teachers will feel respected and appreciated. And," she added, "you'll be amazed at the amount of time that is freed up to engage in what really matters: visionary work." Tim walked away mulling over the idea. It was new and different, but it seemed fairly easy and he decided to give it a try.

Fast-forward four weeks. What started out as a seemingly good plan fell apart quickly. Tim found that a daily email to staff required more effort than he originally thought. He was easily distracted from this task, and even when he wrote the memos, they were often late. Teachers were thankful for the extra time, but within two weeks, complaints of "not knowing what's going on" were beginning to materialize. What's worse, Tim hadn't realized how much of a hands-on manager he liked to be. If he was honest with himself, it was difficult to relinquish that bit of control. The weekly meeting gave him an opportunity to check in with the staff, and without it, he was beginning to feel disconnected. By the third week, he had rescheduled the staff meetings for every Friday morning. Tim had moved from the Unaware stage to the Conscious stage on the Continuum of Self-Reflection. He was aware of a strategy that might bring about better results, but he was unable to implement it consistently and intentionally.

Soon after, Jade called Tim, wanting to follow up on their conversation and see how the new idea was working out. Tim filled her in, slightly embarrassed to admit that he gave up so easily. They agreed to meet and talk later in the week to troubleshoot each of the issues that arose. After that powerful discussion, Tim returned to work with newfound determination to make monthly staff meetings work. He rearranged his morning schedule to make the daily email to staff his first priority. To better keep his finger on the pulse of the school, he began implementing a feedback-rich walk-through regimen every day. His staff appreciated the attention to instruction and the emailed updates, and by the third week of the new routine, Tim was experiencing a feeling of success he'd not felt before. He'd been able to turn new knowledge into consistent action with proven results. Tim had stepped into the Action stage on the Continuum of Self-Reflection.

With increased confidence, Tim began to rethink some of his other basic routines. He and Jade continued to meet each month to talk about time management and share ideas on working with greater efficiency. He began to seek out articles and blogs on the topic and was soon able to distinguish between strategies that would work for his site and those that wouldn't. This sophisticated level of thinking is defined as the Refinement stage on the Continuum of Self-Reflection. Through deliberate thought, intentional action, and an ongoing assessment of his leadership approaches, Tim had utilized the practice of self-reflection to propel himself forward as a leader.

The P-CSR Linked to the Principal Leadership Development Framework

Tim could be any one of us, depending on the position and context of our leadership assignment. As he developed his reflective thought and intentionality, he also partnered with a colleague to deepen his thinking and refine his approaches. Quite directly, his enriched thinking led directly to an increase in his effectiveness.

Figure 2.3 shows how the Principal's Continuum of Self-Reflection aligns with the Principal Leadership Development Framework. The descriptors associated with each stage should be seen more as reference points than as a checklist of behaviors that need to be mastered before advancing to the next stage. In a nutshell, this is a tool that helps leaders identify the depth to which they think about the work they do. Having the descriptors of effective practice, as outlined in the PLDF, is helpful only insofar as to provide a clear target at which to aim. If we are to expect growth toward mastery of these targets by asking "Where am I going?" then we must simultaneously ask "Where am I now?" and "How am I going to get there?" (Stiggins, Arter, Chappuis, & Chappuis, 2004).

The descriptors in each row provide a valuable means to assess an individual's reflective state of mind and to build awareness of specific thoughts and actions that characterize one as a leader. By reading through the leadership descriptors from the Unaware stage to the Refinement stage, a clear path emerges that will guide both thought and action toward becoming a Refinement-stage leader. Chapters 3–6 will delve more deeply into each of the four roles of the building administrator and the criteria that characterize each.

FIGURE 2.3

The P-CSR Linked to the PLDF

PRINCIPAL AS VISIONARY

UNAWARE	CONSCIOUS	ACTION	REFINEMENT
FOCUS ON BUILDING AWARENESS	FOCUS ON PLANNING AND BEING MORE INTENTIONAL	FOCUS ON ACCURATELY ASSESSING THE IMPACT OF ACTIONS	FOCUS ON BECOMING MORE RESPONSIVE
• Lacks understanding or development of personal impact on the school's mission and vision. • Allocates resources and engages in practices without alignment to the school's mission and vision. • May or may not access site needs assessment and/or School Improvement Plan (SIP). • Makes decisions independent of or contrary to the mission and vision.	• Understands the mission and vision of the school. • Addresses situations without overtly connecting the school's data-informed needs of mission and vision. • Takes actions that may or may not take into account the site needs assessment and/or SIP. • Makes decisions that may or may not be aligned with the mission and vision.	• Articulates and communicates the mission and vision of the school. • Aligns school decisions, practices, and resources with the mission and vision. • Promotes the development and application of SIP based on the site needs assessment. • Utilizes the school's mission and vision to provide rationale for actions and decisions.	• Initiates and proactively leads the communication, implementation, and ongoing revision of the school's mission, vision, and SIP. • Weighs and bases all decisions, practices, and resources to implement and sustain the mission, vision, and SIP. • Collaboratively creates, monitors, and refines the SIP based on needs assessment data points. • Compels and partners with constituents to innovate, support, and promote the school's mission and vision.

Continued

PRINCIPAL AS INSTRUCTIONAL LEADER

UNAWARE	CONSCIOUS	ACTION	REFINEMENT
FOCUS ON BUILDING AWARENESS	FOCUS ON PLANNING AND BEING MORE INTENTIONAL	FOCUS ON ACCURATELY ASSESSING THE IMPACT OF ACTIONS	FOCUS ON BECOMING MORE RESPONSIVE
• Has not enacted steps toward developing a PLC. • Adheres to the formal observation process and does not go beyond that. • Maintains status quo regarding curriculum, instruction, and assessment. • Does not understand, access, or use available data.	• Organizes school staff with some elements of PLC present. • Completes the formal evaluation process and may or may not pursue further monitoring of instruction. • Takes steps to update curriculum, instruction, and assessment practices. • Collects data, and may or may not use it to update action plans.	• Facilitates the implementation of the structural elements of a PLC. • Supervises and monitors instruction, providing feedback to teachers. • Coordinates curriculum, instruction, and assessment practices. • Analyzes data to create and refine action plans.	• Builds collective capacity of entire staff through the cultivation of a robust and equitable student-focused PLC. • Builds individual and collective capacity of entire staff through differentiated supervision, coaching, and evaluation practices. • Assures the alignment of curriculum, instruction, and assessment that meet all students' needs. • Promotes monitoring systems that utilize real-time data to inform teams' and teachers' instruction and intervention decisions.

PRINCIPAL AS ENGAGER

UNAWARE	CONSCIOUS	ACTION	REFINEMENT
FOCUS ON BUILDING AWARENESS	FOCUS ON PLANNING AND BEING MORE INTENTIONAL	FOCUS ON ACCURATELY ASSESSING THE IMPACT OF ACTIONS	FOCUS ON BECOMING MORE RESPONSIVE
• Manages the day-to-day operations of the school without emphasis on Whole Child tenets. • Does not seek out opportunities to partner with outside agencies and constituents. • Allows change to halt actions and/or interrupt school operations. • Completes tasks without tending to issues of social justice, equity, and/or diversity. • Does not see a need to cultivate staff as reflective practitioners.	• Demonstrates awareness of Whole Child tenets without specific plans to address them. • Partners with outside constituents on an as-needed or as-requested basis. • Resists change and/or reacts to changing contexts with immediate actions. • Tends to issues of social justice, equity, and diversity as they arise. • Is aware of the need for policies and practices that will cultivate staff as reflective practitioners.	• Enacts structures and procedures to address Whole Child tenets. • Builds relationships with outside agencies and constituents intentionally. • Embraces change as an opportunity to learn and grow. • Implements structures and procedures that celebrate diversity, leverage cultural assets, and provide for equity and social justice within the school. • Collaboratively develops policies and practices that cultivate staff as reflective practitioners.	• Maintains a priority of fostering an environment that tends to Whole Child tenets. • Creates, cultivates, and sustains partnerships with outside agencies and constituents to support the school's mission and vision. • Leads positive change processes by assessing, analyzing, and anticipating emerging trends. • Safeguards community values, displaying an appreciation for diversity and social justice by advocating for all students through equitable education practices. • Leads the implementation of policies and practices that cultivate staff as reflective practitioners.

Continued

PRINCIPAL AS LEARNER & COLLABORATOR

UNAWARE	CONSCIOUS	ACTION	REFINEMENT
• Tends to professional development as an add-on service for staff. • Accepts hierarchical structures and follows established decision-making processes. • Displays actions that do not show attempts to connect with local values, continuous growth, and/or lifelong learning. • Works independently, without seeking support from a Community of Practice or professional learning organization.	• Provides resources in support of professional development endeavors that may or may not relate to mission and vision. • Incorporates some shared decision-making practices and works within the established leadership structures. • Displays actions that may or may not be consistent with local values, continuous growth, and/or lifelong learning for self and staff. • Considers membership in a Community of Practice or professional organization on occasion.	• Arranges professional development opportunities for staff that support the mission, vision, and currently assessed site needs. • Provides opportunities for leaders to emerge through collaborative decision-making structures. • Attempts to model reflective practice, confidence, humility, perseverance, and interest in continuous growth and life-long learning while encouraging staff to do the same. • Accesses colleagues through a Community of Practice, leadership network, or professional learning organization.	• Facilitates the delivery of job-embedded, ongoing professional learning opportunities for self and staff, based on mission, vision, and established site needs, that focus on results. • Develops internal leaders and nurtures a culturally responsive environment of shared ownership and decision making. • Models reflective practice, confidence, humility, perseverance, and interest in continuous growth and lifelong learning. • Participates regularly in a Community of Practice, leadership network, and professional learning organization(s).

FOCUS ON BUILDING AWARENESS

FOCUS ON PLANNING AND BEING MORE INTENTIONAL

FOCUS ON ACCURATELY ASSESSING THE IMPACT OF ACTIONS

FOCUS ON BECOMING MORE RESSPONSIVE

The Reflective Cycle

John Dewey (1910) defined self-reflection as "thinking about one's thinking." If you think of the stages along the Principal's Continuum of Self-Reflection as stops on a long and dusty highway, then the Reflective Cycle (see Figure 2.4) is the vehicle used to get you to your destination: becoming a reflective leader. As you'll see when looking at the continuum, the wheel sometimes starts slowly for folks in the Unaware stage. It may even get stuck a time or two as you pass through the Conscious stage. Eventually, though, it gains traction and picks up speed as it rolls through the Action stage and heads into the Refinement stage, where the reflective leader operates.

Let's zoom in a little bit on the vehicle that propels us forward on this venture. We start by identifying four characteristics (or attributes, behaviors, or habits of mind) that combine to define the behaviors of effective, accurate reflection. These four components (identified in the inner sections of our wheel) are critical to clarifying how we think and how our thinking affects our professional performance.

All leaders demonstrate, to varying degrees, skills and tendencies related to each of four areas: Awareness of Leadership Context, Intentionality of Actions, Ability to Accurately Assess, and Capability to Adjust Actions. These gradients of skill, habits, and reflective accuracy are illustrated on a sliding scale or continuum: the Continuum of Self-Reflection.

Interestingly, growth of self-reflective tendencies tends to follow a repeated (and repeatable) pattern. We have come to call this the Reflective Cycle. A leader must necessarily develop awareness before seeking to act with intentionality, engage in intentional practice prior to assessing the effect of one's actions, and determine impact prior to enacting interventions. The frequency with which a principal engages in the Reflective Cycle will contribute to overarching growth and address the question "How often do I reflect?"

Reflective practitioners have awareness of their leadership context: *How aware am I of the status of learning and teaching in my school, our current reality and needs, and my leadership role?*

Charlotte Danielson (2007) describes awareness as comprehensively "seeing" what's going on. A reflective leader is attentive to every nuance in the building and continually seeks to know more. Keen awareness includes knowledge of student data and patterns, public perception of the school, instructional strengths and weaknesses of staff, and a host of other contextual factors. Reflection is a way of "taking stock" of "the mental models and accompanying actions that leaders need to access" (Childs-Bowen, 2007b)—including the principal's ability to influence all of the aforementioned elements through leadership behaviors, words, and deeds.

Reflective practitioners are intentional in their actions: *How intentionally do I align decisions, actions, policies, and resources to meet our needs?*

FIGURE 2.4

The Reflective Cycle for Principals

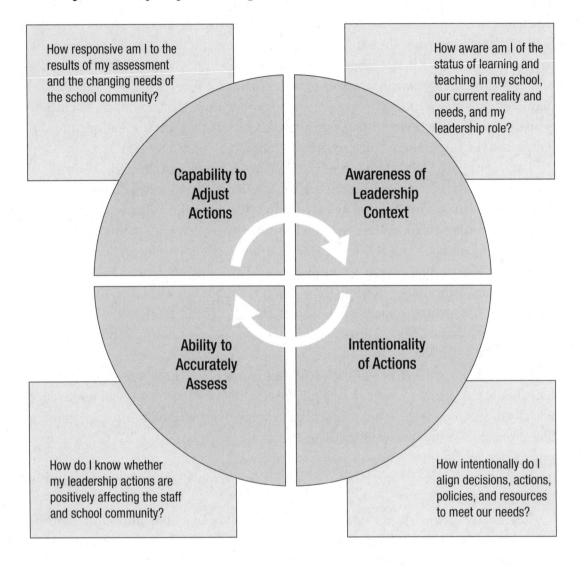

How responsive am I to the results of my assessment and the changing needs of the school community?

How aware am I of the status of learning and teaching in my school, our current reality and needs, and my leadership role?

Capability to Adjust Actions

Awareness of Leadership Context

Ability to Accurately Assess

Intentionality of Actions

How do I know whether my leadership actions are positively affecting the staff and school community?

How intentionally do I align decisions, actions, policies, and resources to meet our needs?

With awareness of the instructional reality, a leader can better identify necessary School Improvement Plan (SIP) goals; select curricula, materials, and professional development targets; make decisions regarding staff assignments; revise schoolwide policies; and implement structural procedures to best meet the specific needs of the building. All decisions and actions are weighed and made with a strategic purpose. Believing "what gets planned gets done," reflective leaders take the time to plan their actions—and follow their plans.

Reflective practitioners accurately assess their impact: *How do I know whether my leadership actions are positively affecting the staff and school community?*

Once a leader engages in intentional, calculated actions, it is imperative to determine whether or not the specific actions result in the intended outcomes. Engaging in some form of assessment is the next step on the reflective cycle. Assessment tools are wide-ranging and implemented based on situation and need: walkthroughs, perception surveys, various student achievement measures, attendance and behavioral queries, instructional audit data, and other methods of data collection inform the leader of the degree to which his or her actions are positively affecting the staff and school community.

Reflective practitioners adjust their actions as necessary: *How responsive am I to the results of my assessment and the changing needs of the school community?*

In the Reflective Cycle, leaders armed with real-time assessment data can immediately adapt their approach, modify a decision, or even stop and regroup. These actions—based on ongoing, formative assessment information—help clarify misconceptions, recalibrate energy, increase engagement, and provide an alternative method for helping both staff and students succeed. Highly reflective leaders know they have a powerful and immediate effect on the entire school community; thus they are always on the lookout for opportunities to leverage that impact in positive, supportive ways.

Reflective practitioners engage in ongoing reflection: *How often do I reflect?*

Reflection is a habit; as such, it must be developed. Engaging in the Reflective Cycle requires practice, diligence, and focus. Reflective practitioners have mastered this process and seem to engage in ongoing reflection almost intuitively. They do not wait for someone to pose a reflective prompt or suggest that they attend to something. Rather, they are constantly alert to the reality of their buildings, making decisions intentionally, assessing the impact of those decisions, and taking immediate actions to course correct as necessary (Hall & Simeral, 2015).

Heading Toward Refinement-Stage Leadership

Our reflective tendencies are fluid. As we develop and strengthen our skills and habits, we flow along the Principal's Continuum of Self-Reflection—with an end goal of reaching the Refinement stage, which is characterized by constant thought and continuous reflection. There is no finish line, just movement toward a pattern of thinking that leads to more effective professional practice. With concerted effort and consistent, individualized, differentiated support, we can usher our principals toward this goal. As expert school leader and author Thomas Hoerr so aptly reminds us, there is an art to leadership: "Strong leaders are artists because they recognize that there is no one formula, no particular policy, no set of procedures that will always work with everyone or, even, will always work with any one person" (2005, p. 1).

PART II

Building Principal Leadership Capacity

As you enter Part II of this resource, you are preparing to take action. You have a thorough understanding of the four roles of instructional leadership and the criteria for success, as outlined in the Principal Leadership Development Framework (PLDF). You see the Principal's Continuum of Self-Reflection (P-CSR) embedded within the Framework, describing the link between our thinking and our actions. You have the Reflective Cycle at your disposal, enabling you to focus your reflective energy toward the cultivation of more effective leadership behaviors. And now, we provide you with actionable strategies to build your reflective habits—and your instructional leadership effectiveness.

In Chapters 3–6, each of the 17 criteria from the PLDF is explained in greater detail. Accompanying each criterion is a guiding question—most assuredly one that school leaders face on a regular basis—that prompts further discussion. In response to each question, we have identified a theory of action. Stacey Childress and her colleagues at Harvard University describe a theory of action as a representation of "the organization's collective belief about the causal relationships between certain actions and desired outcomes" (Childress, Johnson, Elmore, & Grossman, 2007, p. 45). For instance, we believe teachers are the primary determinant of student success. Therefore, our theory of action might be this: *If we allocate our resources to building teachers' instructional capacity, then our teachers will become more effective in raising student achievement throughout our school system.*

We've offered two high-leverage strategies for each criterion, selecting those that are most actionable and lead most directly to enhanced leadership performance. Many strategies also include tools, templates, protocols, and forms (found in Appendix B and available online at www.ascd.org/ASCD/pdf/books/TPI2016.pdf.

Remember, this isn't just for principals—it's for anyone in a leadership position at the school or district level. If you are a building-level leader, focus your attention on the strategies listed in Pathway One (i.e., at the school level). If you supervise principals or support the leadership development from the district level, orient your focus on the strategies listed in Pathway Two (i.e., at the district level). Keep in mind that many of the strategies are interchangeable and easily adapted or modified to meet your (or your organization's) needs. We encourage you to be creative, keep an open mind, and embrace the possibilities that are contained herein.

We've also sprinkled in some case studies to bring the 17 criteria from the PLDF to life. These are simply profiles of educators, just like you, who have focused their thinking and their actions on identifiable outcomes related to each of the criteria. Taken from a field of educators at many positions within the educational system, these case studies should help illustrate some of the various strategies they have implemented to meet the criteria in the PLDF.

As you read Chapters 3–6, you'll be inspired to implement certain strategies that lead to enhanced leadership growth. With each strategy you select, use the Focused Reflection Questions (Figure A) to focus your efforts and build your reflective capacity as a building leader.

FIGURE A

Focused Reflection Questions

- If operating in the **Unaware stage** in a particular criterion, then in order to grow as a reflective leader, **focus on building awareness** of the leader's role within that criterion, through the strategies outlined within each section. Ask yourself:
    - What is the goal you are trying to accomplish?
    - How might this strategy help you accomplish the goal?
    - How is this strategy different than what you typically do?
    - Without implementing this strategy, what is the current state of affairs?

- If operating in the **Conscious stage** in a particular criterion, then in order to grow as a reflective leader, **focus on planning and being more intentional** with leadership actions within that criterion, through the strategies outlined within each section. Ask yourself:
    - How will you begin the implementation of this strategy?
    - What is your time frame for beginning (and referring back to) this strategy?
    - How does this fit into your long-range plan for the school?
    - Who will you collaborate with to revise and refine your plan?

- If operating in the **Action stage** in a particular criterion, then in order to grow as a reflective leader, **focus on accurately assessing the impact of actions** within that criterion, through the strategies outlined within each section. Ask yourself:
    - Did your initial implementation of the strategy yield the result you intended?
    - How do you know? What metrics are you using to determine effectiveness?
    - Were there parts of the strategy that were more successful than others?
    - Why was the strategy successful (or not)? What causes can you pinpoint?

- If operating in the **Refinement stage** in a particular criterion, then in order to grow as a reflective leader, **focus on becoming more responsive** to the changing dynamics of the school environment within that criterion, through the strategies outlined within each section. Ask yourself:
    - When did you first notice the impact (positive, negative, or neutral) of this strategy?
    - How did you respond to that information?
    - How can you keep yourself aware of short-term *and* long-term goals as you're planning the implementation of this strategy?
    - How could you adapt the strategy to better meet your goal(s)?

Remember, the P-CSR and the Reflective Cycle are tools designed to guide and support growth on the PLDF. If we are to succeed as leaders, we must seek to develop and increase our capacity through reflection and simultaneous action. To be sure, we ask you to keep in mind Paulo Friere, an influential Brazilian educator and theorist who reminded us "that reflection and action must never be undertaken independently" (Freire, 1970).

CHAPTER 3
Principal as Visionary

The vision is the compass by which we sail our ship, and the School Improvement Plan (SIP) is the map that outlines the path to our destination. Without a vision, we may have a boatload of loyal, hard-working sailors covering a lot of territory, but we won't necessarily be able to tell if we're heading in the right direction or making progress toward our goals.

There are four criteria within the PLDF for the principal who serves as Visionary. Each is described in greater depth below, and strategies for building leadership capacity within each criterion complete the chapter.

- Criterion 1: Articulates, communicates, and leads the collaborative implementation and ongoing revision of the school's mission and vision.
- Criterion 2: Aligns and bases all decisions, practices, policies, and resources (e.g., human capital, time, budgetary, and facilities) on the school's mission and vision.
- Criterion 3: Promotes the collaborative creation, monitoring, and refinement of short- and long-term school improvement plans.
- Criterion 4: Compels the district and school community to embrace and work toward the attainment of the shared mission and vision.

Criterion 1: Articulates, communicates, and leads the collaborative implementation and ongoing revision of the school's mission and vision

Before a ship can set sail, the captain must have a clear and compelling vision for the voyage. Seated principals have an immense challenge: they must set the course while the ship is already sailing! In order to maintain a proper heading, all stakeholders (community members, local businesses, parents, students, staff, and others) must share in the understanding and creation of that vision. Effective visionary leaders shepherd that network of stakeholders through the process of crafting and revising the school's mission, vision, and SIP—they cannot do it on their own. "A principal's vision, standing alone, needs to be 'sold' and 'bought into.' By contrast, a shared vision based upon the core values of the participants and their hopes for the school ensures commitment to its realization" (Lambert, 2003, p. 6). We agree that "great leaders rally people to a better future" using "a vivid image of what the future could hold" to motivate, guide, escort, and compel stakeholders toward that vision (Buckingham, 2005, p. 59).

VISIONARY LEADERSHIP IN ACTION

Cornerstone Learning Community, a preK–8 school in Tallahassee, Florida, was born from a desire to create a joyful learning experience for children, and this vision is intertwined in every element of the school. In 2000, Jason Flom participated in the creation of the community, helping parents and staff address the question "What does a school look, feel, and act like if its central mission is to foster a lifelong love of learning?" As a result, the school community's families and staff, working together, zeroed in on the one thing most essential to their work: to nurture and respect the integrity of the Whole Child.

This focus now guides all meetings and filters ideas, initiatives, and evaluation of school programs. To keep the vision alive, Flom leads the staff in asking the question "Is what we are spending our time on contributing to our 'one thing'?" As the building leader, he is also focused on the adult learners. Framing decisions and actions to ignite and sustain the teachers' passion to learn, Flom shares, "If teachers are whole learners themselves, then that vigorous learning will lead to Whole Child learning in the classroom."

District-level leaders are ultimately responsible for their principals' ability to cultivate a strong, shared vision for their schools. Through coaching and various direct activities, supervisors and district officials can engage principals in the practice of clarifying their vision, developing a concise vision statement, and reflecting collaboratively on strategies to partner with their constituents. Connected to this work are the professional learning and support necessary to construct (and continuously revise as a "living document") a focused SIP that aligns with the shared vision. Vision is a simultaneously top-down and bottom-up (and side-to-side) construct, which necessitates that all stakeholders—especially its leaders and future leaders within the system—have the skills, opportunity, and reflective ability to develop as Visionary leaders.

Criterion 2: Aligns and bases all decisions, practices, policies, and resources (e.g., human capital, time, budgetary, and facilities) on the school's mission and vision

Having a clear and compelling vision is only as useful as it is utilized. This criterion is where principals really must show determination in stewarding the vision. With enthusiasm, tenacity, and resolve, visionary leaders rally the crew around a common focus and use the SIP as a map—the navigational chart—for engaging in the work. From hiring practices to teaching assignments, from budget planning to expense approvals, from master schedules to professional development, every allocated resource—and every action the principal takes—must lead the school community one step closer to the goal(s). "If not, they know (recognize, reflect, and act) that they may need to redefine their use of these resources" (Childs-Bowen, 2007a).

Visionary principals are tasked with seeding that shared vision among all stakeholders while simultaneously transforming the school community in pursuit of the vision. In addition, building leaders are responsible for ensuring that all of the oarsmen (to continue the sailing ship metaphor) see themselves as viable contributors to the attainment of the collective vision—in other words, the staff must row in unison in order to help sustain forward momentum (Jenkins, 2008).

Support from the district office can help principals utilize their four greatest resources: personnel, time, finances, and facilities. By providing opportunities for leaders to collaborate, discuss their SIPs and strategies, analyze data, and evaluate the allocation of resources, district officials can facilitate the learning necessary to keep the daily work aligned to long-term targets. One major factor that supports fidelity to the SIP (and the DIP: District Improvement Plan) is that the district remains "relentless about its purpose" (Jenkins, 2008). Equipped with an understanding of the district's consistent vision and strategic priorities, building leaders are readied to consider the implications for the individual school vision. Including assistant principals and aspiring principals in these analyses helps maintain their fidelity to the SIP and prepare them to be visionary leaders anywhere within the school system.

VISIONARY LEADERSHIP IN ACTION

The vision statement in the Cypress-Fairbanks Independent School District (outside Houston, TX) is bold and emphatic: "Learn. Empower. Achieve. Dream. LEAD." As the director for staff development, Glenda Horner's charge is to provide staff with the knowledge, tools, and skills necessary to attain that vision. In order to maintain alignment with the vision, Horner emphasizes three critical dimensions in her work:

knowing the people, connecting them with a sense of purpose, and continuously improving all processes. Each is woven carefully and purposefully into the fabric of her work, whether it is planning and facilitating professional development, guiding a committee, or informing district procedures. If the means don't lead to the agreed-upon end, then the project must be reevaluated. Horner believes this emphasis plays a crucial role in connecting personnel with the vision. Ultimately, that vision will inform their decisions and help accomplish their outcomes. If the data are any indication, the outcomes are matching the vision. The district—with more than 112,000 students—is the largest in Texas to have 100% of its campuses earn Met Standard honors on the 2014 Texas Education Agency accountability ratings.

Criterion 3: Promotes the collaborative creation, monitoring, and refinement of short- and long-term school improvement plans

In *Alice's Adventures in Wonderland*, Alice asks the Cheshire Cat for directions:

> "Would you tell me, please, which way I ought to go from here?"

> "That depends a good deal on where you want to get to," said the Cat. (Carroll, 1865)

On the open seas, raising the sail and catching wind will move the boat, but to what end? With a thoroughly mapped journey, principals significantly increase the likelihood that their schools will achieve their collective vision. The School Improvement Plan provides the necessary heading. This tool—a concise document expressing intended outcomes, strategies, timelines, and specific action steps—is the map for all stakeholders to follow. Leading the collaborative construction of an SIP that aligns with the vision, matches site needs, and is supported by data and research enables principals to ensure that all of the school's work is oriented toward the vision of student success. Indeed, maintaining laserlike focus is a key responsibility of leadership, described as "the extent to which the leader establishes clear goals and keeps those goals in the forefront of the school's attention" (Marzano et al., 2005, p. 50). Assistant principals, aspiring principals, and other stakeholders often contribute to the development, monitoring, and refinement of the SIP—making even more compelling the argument for explicitly communicating the vision.

VISIONARY LEADERSHIP IN ACTION

Often, staff members become so consumed with their day-to-day challenges that their connection to the vision and SIP weakens. At a large high school in the Los Angeles area, this is precisely when coauthor Ann Cunningham-Morris stepped in. As an assistant principal, she volunteered to cochair the building's School Improvement Team, recruiting teacher leaders and family/community leaders to provide input and serve as liaisons with stakeholder groups.

Once a solid SIP was in place, the challenge of connecting the daily grind to the long-term goals became evident. Very intentionally, Cunningham-Morris guided the staff through an ongoing process to frame all work involving the school—including teaching and learning, day-to-day operations, extracurricular activities, and parent/family and community engagement strategies. The goals and related actions of the SIP were always in the forefront of communication, decision making, and problem solving for all groups addressing the "business" of the school.

On a quarterly basis, Cunningham-Morris brought the School Improvement Team together to collect feedback, analyze data, celebrate successes, and determine what changes were in order—all of which were shared with the school's stakeholders. As a result of this consistent focus, Cunningham-Morris explains, "We didn't jump from one initiative to another—we stuck with the plan. Soon everyone in the community was literally on the same page." Not surprisingly, the results included heightened student achievement and increased teacher retention.

At the district level, SIPs are often scrutinized for clarity, alignment, and research-based strategies. Involving principals in collective exploration of model plans, work sessions to lead collaborative protocols, and frequent analysis of the SIPs themselves can help the efficacy of the plans. This sort of high-stakes strategic planning is often overlooked in principal preparation programs (Hess & Kelly, 2005); thus it becomes the district's obligation to provide that support and professional development. Such collaborative work would include an investigation of vertical alignment (between schools and the district) and horizontal alignment (among schools), supporting the viability of the district's short-term and long-term vision.

Criterion 4: Compels the district and school community to embrace and work toward the attainment of the shared mission and vision

As school leaders know all too well, change happens. And when the winds shift, the current alters and other forces affect forward progress. These forces present a challenge to change or even abandon a vision for one that might appear easier to attain. Principals know the importance of adopting a well-defined decision-making process at the beginning of any planning or implementation process. The visionary principal's passion, contagious to all stakeholders, is demonstrated through unwavering commitment to the vision and SIP—those elements that serve as the institution's "true north" (George, 2007).

It is important to note that fidelity to the vision and blind adherence to any given strategy are different—the former is essential, and the latter can be dangerous. Visionary principals understand the need to modify the plan, make course corrections, and innovate in order to meet the changing conditions. All stakeholders, if firmly on board with the vision and SIP, will likewise use the vision as a guidepost—or a lighthouse—for decision making.

VISIONARY LEADERSHIP IN ACTION

At Hayah International Academy in Cairo, Egypt, a concerted effort to create an equitable, Whole Child–focused educational system created an unintended wrinkle. After bringing a doctor on campus, offering religious classes, providing character education, and making multiple wraparound services available for students, many teachers began to delegate portions of the Whole Child education to the specialists. That's where Amanda Romey, the school's assistant principal, stepped in. Emphasizing the interdependence among all of the adults' roles, Romey led discussions with the staff that harkened back to the original vision.

From these conversations came new cross-curricular connections, collaborative planning, and the collective "ownership" of all of the school's students. Now, the expectation is that learning in character education classes should affect students' behavior in other classes, on the soccer pitch, and in the community. Staff are beginning to watch for—and demand—those connections.

With the keen eyes of the staff turning toward student outcomes across content and grade levels, the staff is more attuned to individual students' needs, strengths, and gaps. "Now," says Romey, "our focus is on creating an environment where kids feel safe to take learning risks: asking the right questions is more important than providing the right answers."

District office leadership can support principals' effectiveness in this criterion by providing ongoing learning opportunities that emphasize decision-making approaches. Since this criterion is all about execution in the eye of the storm, it would behoove district officials to confirm that their principals are equipped with multiple decision-making strategies, can provide a rationale for their decisions, maintain their bearings in challenging situations, and remain focused on the shared vision . . . while maintaining strong professional partnerships with all stakeholder groups. Including assistant principals and other site-based leaders in this process offers the district a pipeline of leaders who have a solid repertoire of decision-making strategies to implement as visionary leaders.

Growing as a Visionary Leader: Strategies for Reflective Growth

In the following sections, we offer several strategies for building principals' leadership capacity within this role. Each provides the opportunity for the principal (Pathway One) and the district-level supervisors (Pathway Two) to clarify the work and streamline all efforts toward the long-term outcome: develop and refine reflective practices while simultaneously augmenting expertise in these criteria. Simply put, we're aiming for principals to operate in the Refinement stage as visionary leaders.

The strategies we offer are but a sampling of the many avenues to approach growth within each criterion (see Figure 3.1). The strategies we have selected deliver high-leverage, universal results, and many of them include tools, templates, protocols, and forms you can find in Appendix B and online at www.ascd.org/ASCD/pdf/books/TPI2016.pdf. It is our intent to provide immediately actionable, easily implemented strategies that bridge the gap between research and application. Strategies with a support resource in Appendix B are marked with an asterisk (*).

With a thorough understanding of the role and criteria that contribute to effective instructional leadership within the role of a visionary leader, a good place to begin is with an honest self-assessment. Reflect on each criterion as a separate piece of your leadership puzzle. Within each criterion, we have added a brief self-assessment guide to facilitate leaders' exploration of their current thinking and technical proficiency. In the Reflective Leadership Planning Template (found in Appendix A and downloadable at www.ascd.org/ASCD/pdf/books/TPI2016.pdf), we suggest that principals (or assistant principals or aspiring principals) sit down with their supervisors/mentors/coaches and

FIGURE 3.1

Principal as Visionary Strategy Schematic

	CRITERION 1: Articulates, communicates, and leads the collaborative implementation and ongoing revision of the school's mission and vision	CRITERION 2: Aligns and bases all decisions, practices, policies, and resources (e.g., human capital, time, budgetary, and facilities) on the school's mission and vision	CRITERION 3: Promotes the collaborative creation, monitoring, and refinement of short- and long-term school improvement plans	CRITERION 4: Compels the district and school community to embrace and work toward the attainment of the shared mission and vision
PATHWAY ONE: SCHOOL LEVEL	• Prepare an Elevator Speech* • Maximize Social Media* • Connect the Dots*	• Create a Synergistic Schematic • Initiate a Resource Audit*	• Map the Plan Together • Monitor Data Collaboratively • Continuously Reflect and Assess Stakeholder Concerns*	• Clarify Group Parameters* • Filter Decisions
PATHWAY TWO: DISTRICT LEVEL	• Systematize a Theory of Action • Establish a Proactive Transition Plan*	• Lead Collaborative Data-Driven Dialogues* • Build Budget Literacy*	• Clarify Vertical Alignment* • Tune Plans in a Principal-PLC* • Embrace Continuous Improvement*	• Expand Their Toolkits* • Navigate Difficult Situations*

Note: Strategies with an asterisk (*) include a tool/template/protocol/form in Appendix B.

collaboratively record a narrative of their own current reality, including where they operate on the Principal's Continuum of Self-Reflection.

After scrutinizing the sample strategies that follow and collaboratively brainstorming additional strategies (with colleagues, supervisors, and others in your professional learning network), use the Reflective Leadership Planning Template to document the powerful steps you will take to develop your (or your principal's) growth as a reflective instructional leader. There is great strength in the dialogue, collaboration, and partnership in this goal-setting endeavor; utilize the resources at your disposal to create and refine a clear, focused, reflection-oriented plan.

Criterion 1

Guiding Question: How can we get everybody on board?

Theory of Action: The principal is the figurehead of the school and is responsible for garnering complete and unilateral support for the difficult work of school improvement. Often, this requires adaptive work—the learning required to diminish the gap between vision and reality (Heifetz, 1994). If the principal initiates and proactively leads the communication, implementation, and ongoing revision of the school's mission, vision, and SIP, then all stakeholders will see themselves as co-owners and viable contributors to the accomplishment of their common goal(s).

In Figure 3.2, the Principal's Continuum of Self-Reflection describes the depth of thinking related to leadership actions in this criterion. To the right of each stage is the focus behavior for developing reflective capacity within the criterion. Refer to the Reflective Cycle (Figure 2.3, p. 17) and the focused reflective questions (Figure 2.4, p. 22) for more guidance.

FIGURE 3.2

P-CSR: *Visionary Criterion 1*

UNAWARE STAGE	BUILD AWARENESS	CONSCIOUS STAGE	PLAN INTENTIONALLY	ACTION STAGE	ACCURATELY ASSESS IMPACT	REFINEMENT STAGE	BECOME RESPONSIVE
Lacks understanding or development of personal impact on the school's mission and vision.		Understands the mission and vision of the school.		Articulates and communicates the mission and vision of the school.		Initiates and proactively leads the communication, implementation, and ongoing revision of the school's mission, vision, and SIP.	

Pathway One: School Level

Prepare an Elevator Speech*

An elevator speech is a brief statement about the school's mission and vision, their importance, and how they might be attained. Work to hone this statement into a two-minute (or shorter) spiel, rehearsing and modeling the process with stakeholders.

At its core, an elevator speech serves several purposes: it is a communication tool, helping to articulate a vision and its importance; it is a sales tool, garnering followers; and it is a teaching tool, used to build stakeholder understanding and support toward collaborative implementation.

An elevator speech can be used with potential donors, volunteers, partners, community members, colleagues, staff members, and people outside the field of education. With a catchy, powerful, succinct elevator speech at the ready, school leaders can convey the mission and vision to anyone at any time. See Appendix B.1 for guidelines in formulating and refining an elevator speech.

Maximize Social Media*

Smartphones, tablets, apps, scrolling feeds, alerts, and social media channels provide quick and rather simple access to students, parents, community members, and school partners. School leaders can benefit from this digital savviness by ramping up their communication strategies; principals have a unique vantage to delve into this arena. Connecting with stakeholders, especially to convey the school's mission and vision, is a key part of a school's communication plan. With technology at our fingertips, we can—and many stakeholders expect that we will—share news, updates, changes, and images immediately.

Using platforms such as Facebook, Twitter, Instagram, and the school website, principals can bring the vision to life in real time. They can share highlights, messages, inspirational quotes, upcoming events, and photos that support the collective vision. Using the Customized Strategic Communication Plan (Appendix B.2), principals can view examples and create a plan to maximize these digital resources. Principals will find this tool helpful as they integrate communication aspects into the SIP to support monitoring and revision strategies.

Connect the Dots*

Involving all stakeholders in the creation, implementation, and revision of the SIP can enrich the plan tremendously. However, some stakeholders are infrequently available, though they may have a unique and profound impact on the school community. For example, athletic coaches affect many students on an individual and collective basis and serve as representatives of the school (and its vision) with parents, spectators, and students and officials from neighboring schools—yet some are not full-time employees of the school, so they may not join certain meetings. Principals can increase the connectivity of these stakeholders to the vision by inviting certain groups, such as support staff, extracurricular activity leaders, athletic coaches, and other school partners, to a special meeting at the beginning of the year. Using the Triad Protocol (Appendix B.3) in this initial meeting and in quarterly follow-up meetings will help develop strategic moves, gather feedback, and institutionalize the vision. As they collaboratively unpack the vision and connect it to their roles, responsibilities, and expected behaviors, even "part-time" stakeholders can begin to leverage their effect on the accomplishment of the collective goal(s).

Pathway Two: District Level

Systematize a Theory of Action

The district vision can be a handy resource for central office supervisors to engage principals in collaborative conversations regarding the alignment of their school visions. This process begins with broad-based coherence of the district's Theory of Action. A theory of action represents the district's collective belief in the causal relationships of certain actions and desired outcomes. To develop a districtwide theory of action, supervisors will engage principals in a series of *if-then* prompts, such as:

> If Central Office does _____, then principals will _____, which will
> assist teachers to _____, which will help students to _____.

Although the development of a clear theory of action is a product of these conversations, the real value rests in the coherence of principals across the district as they develop or refine their schools' visions aligned to the district's vision and theory of action.

Establish a Proactive Transition Plan*

With a change in building leadership comes anxiety and wonder. What will the new principal's vision be? What will become of the current vision? Does the arrival of a new principal automatically signify an impending change of the school's vision? District officials can ensure that the transition adds confidence, validity, and forward momentum by clarifying their goals, communicating the vision, and hiring principals proactively. Creating a detailed transition plan that includes stakeholder feedback, considers internal and external candidates, communicates with the school community throughout the process, and ensures the maintenance or reestablishment of a collective vision helps to alleviate local stress in leadership changes.

By surveying all invested stakeholders through community forums, online questionnaires, or designated meetings (see Appendix B.4), district officials can get a pulse of the community's commitment to the current vision. The data collected can inform and direct the district's plan for assigning a new principal to the building—including providing guidance regarding expectations for the abandonment or continuation of work toward the school community's vision. This transparency will help guide new leaders and enhance stakeholder buy-in during the transition period.

Criterion 2

Guiding Question: How can we make sure all of our work is oriented toward our vision and goal(s)?

Theory of Action: Common sense tells us that in order to achieve a specified outcome, we must engage in means that lead to that end. To truly achieve success, we must work with laserlike precision, and that includes removing tasks, structures, and actions that are not directly correlated to the achievement of our goal (Reeves, 2002). If the principal weighs and bases all decisions, practices, and resources to implement and sustain the mission, vision, and SIP, then the school is more likely to meet its common goal(s).

In Figure 3.3, the Principal's Continuum of Self-Reflection describes the depth of thinking related to leadership actions in this criterion. To the right of each stage is the focus behavior for developing reflective capacity within the criterion. Refer to the Reflective Cycle (Figure 2.3, p. 17) and the focused reflective questions (Figure 2.4, p. 22) for more guidance.

FIGURE 3.3

P-CSR: Visionary Criterion 2

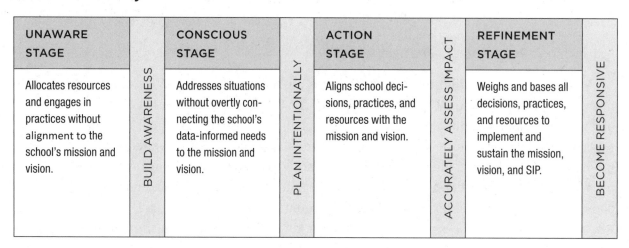

UNAWARE STAGE	BUILD AWARENESS	CONSCIOUS STAGE	PLAN INTENTIONALLY	ACTION STAGE	ACCURATELY ASSESS IMPACT	REFINEMENT STAGE	BECOME RESPONSIVE
Allocates resources and engages in practices without alignment to the school's mission and vision.		Addresses situations without overtly connecting the school's data-informed needs to the mission and vision.		Aligns school decisions, practices, and resources with the mission and vision.		Weighs and bases all decisions, practices, and resources to implement and sustain the mission, vision, and SIP.	

Pathway One: School Level

Create a Synergistic Schematic

Educators' plates are like a smorgasbord, full to overflowing with multiple programs, changing curricula, various materials, shifting expectations, updated research, increasing demands, and day-to-day challenges. From a teacher's point of view, these can often appear to be disjointed and result in well-intentioned conversations that are received as just another thing to pile on an already full plate. Principals can create coherence for teaching staff by helping them see the interconnectivity of their work.

First, principals and their leadership teams can guide teachers to develop a schematic (or some sort of nonlinguistic representation) of how various school practices and approaches support the vision. A potential outcome of this first step is the identification of aspects that do not further the school's work toward the vision and therefore need to be removed from teachers' plates. Then the principal and leadership team can engage the staff in noting the many threads that connect and build interdependence between and among initiatives and approaches throughout the building. This step includes having staff see themselves as viable and contributing members to the attainment of the common goal(s)—and as synergistic resources for one another.

Initiate a Resource Audit*

Some of the principal's greatest external assets—human capital, time, and finances—act as currency in achieving the effective outcomes of the vision. As principals and their stakeholders implement programs, procedures, and practices to support the SIP, it is essential to spend that currency wisely. Monitoring the allocation and utilization of these resources on an ongoing basis helps provide clarity of purpose, rationale for decision making, and justification for action (or nonaction). The Auditing Our Resources template (Appendix B.5) can serve as a guide for principals and stakeholders as they conduct quarterly resource audits—intentional analyses of expenditures—to stay on track and act with transparency.

Pathway Two: District Level

Lead Collaborative Data-Driven Dialogues*

District-level supervisors can facilitate a laserlike focus on aligning the school vision to the district vision through the use of data in cohorts. These cohorts—groupings of schools with common grade levels, by cluster feeding patterns or other contextual needs—allow principals and leadership teams to collaborate, investigate, challenge, and support one another. Engaging principals in cohorts effectively builds trust and invites transparency, peer coaching, questioning, reflection, and the revision of their visions and SIPs to ensure alignment. Providing data to principals is a helpful first step, and offering tools to analyze and act on the data is a powerful next step. Using protocols such as the Data-Driven Dialogue Standard (Appendix B.6) allows principals to take deep dives, comparing and contrasting data sets from similar sites, collaboratively investigate and problem solve, and generate intentional action plans. District-level leaders can build time into leadership meetings to examine, analyze, and "game plan" with real-time, school-based data, viewed through the lens of the SIPs.

Build Budget Literacy*

School finance is one of the primary resources at a leader's disposal, so it would behoove principals to bolster their skills in leveraging their financial resources to support their school's practices. District officials (e.g., supervisors and financial operations officers) can help build principals' financial literacy by engaging them in quarterly reviews and resource allocation analyses using tools such as the Money Talks Running Record (Appendix B.7). This tool helps principals analyze expenses to determine their effect on SIP goals and articulate the school's specific needs. Utilizing this strategy within cohorts or small groups of principals will further diversify the options available to principals for addressing particular elements of the SIP in a financially responsible manner. The mutual benefit for supervisors and principals is the ability to apply this tool—and the data it provides—to inform future decision making and budgetary allocations at the school and district level.

Criterion 3

Guiding Question: How can we set and maintain an appropriate course?

Theory of Action: The School Improvement Plan should guide all of the work within the building. Effective SIPs meet building needs, are based on research-supported strategies, and are monitored and modified as needed (Boudett, City, & Murnane, 2005). If the principal collaboratively creates, monitors, and refines the SIP based on needs assessment data points, then the plan will always lead toward the accomplishment of the common goal(s).

In Figure 3.4, the Principal's Continuum of Self-Reflection describes the depth of thinking related to leadership actions in this criterion. To the right of each stage is the focus behavior for developing reflective capacity within the criterion. Refer to the Reflective Cycle (Figure 2.3, p. 17) and the focused reflective questions (Figure 2.4, p. 22) for more guidance.

Pathway One: School Level

Map the Plan Together

Created in isolation, an SIP is simply one person's wish list. Built collaboratively, though, it becomes a powerful vehicle for effective, enduring change. Legendary UCLA

FIGURE 3.4

P-CSR: *Visionary Criterion 3*

UNAWARE STAGE	BUILD AWARENESS	CONSCIOUS STAGE	PLAN INTENTIONALLY	ACTION STAGE	ACCURATELY ASSESS IMPACT	REFINEMENT STAGE	BECOME RESPONSIVE
May or may not access site needs assessment and/or School Improvement Plan.		Takes actions that may or may not take into account the site needs assessment and/or SIP.		Promotes the development and application of SIP based on the site needs assessment.		Collaboratively creates, monitors, and refines the SIP based on needs assessment data points.	

basketball coach John Wooden reminds us that "failing to prepare is preparing to fail" (Wooden & Jamison, 2004). This wisdom certainly applies to a well-facilitated school improvement planning process. The leader's effectiveness is increased by using a flow map, mind map, or other graphic representation of the SIP process to help involved stakeholders visualize the pursuit of the collective school vision. Diagrams that include the strategic action steps also alert stakeholders to potential obstacles along the way, helping to create proactive response plans for various contingencies.

Effective visionary principals engage these stakeholders at multiple points during SIP development, revisiting the SIP on a regular basis and revising it as necessary. Used consistently, this strategy invites discourse, addresses multiple viewpoints, offers clarity, and welcomes productive change—all valuable assets to mobilizing a collective school community toward the vision.

Monitor Data Collaboratively

Education is a results-oriented business. As such, it is essential to define the metrics that will determine the effectiveness of any strategy, approach, or goal within the SIP. Researchers from Harvard University suggest we use short-term, medium-term, and long-term data points to answer this question: Are we making progress toward our goals? (Boudett et al., 2005). Long-term data points (e.g., annual proficiency exams) inform the school community of the school's progress toward the vision and overall SIP; medium-term data points (e.g., quarterly benchmark assessment results) provide feedback along the way; and short-term data points (e.g., classroom-based formative assessments) show the immediate effect of initial approaches.

Each offers particular value, and each enables principals, leadership teams, staff, and stakeholders to analyze current performance and determine progress toward the

SIP goal(s) by asking if the strategies are working. If so, to what extent? What might we modify to obtain greater results? How might we engage in that work? In this manner, the ongoing collection and analysis of data guides the continuous revision and refinement of the SIP and its associated action plans.

Continuously Reflect and Assess Stakeholder Concerns*

With a draft of the SIP in hand, convening a representative group of teacher leaders, students, parents, community members, and other stakeholders to self-assess and discuss implementation concerns can be helpful to the overall SIP process. Each group answers a set of questions and reflects on their individual concerns at periodic stages during the implementation of the plan. Using the Stages of Concern tool, part of the Concerns-Based Adoption Model from SEDL (Appendix B.8), building leaders can facilitate the self-assessment sessions using the data from these tools to build reflection among stakeholders.

These data can further assist by extending stakeholder dialogue around questions such as the following: What am I currently doing to support this work? What evidence or results do I have at this point? What support do I need? Are there adequate resources at the school and classroom level to enable me to achieve this outcome? In what ways do we each contribute to the collective accomplishment of our SIP goals?

With this type of continuous reflective practice, principals lead the group in refining their implementation efforts and identifying ways in which groups' interdependence is critical to the overall success of SIP outcomes.

Pathway Two: District Level

Clarify Vertical Alignment*

In a coherent school system, all of the work leads to the accomplishment of shared goals. Effective visionary leaders ensure that the vision, mission, and SIP are aligned vertically between the district and school. Principals' supervisors can provide district-level information—a district improvement plan (DIP), strategic action steps, key district-level data—to display (and refine) the relationships between school and district plans.

Following the Protocol for Clarifying DIP and SIP Alignment (Appendix B.9) helps to link the plans and show connectivity, and it offers a venue for discovering when plans and goals are out of alignment—creating an opportunity for principals and their supervisors to adjust and refine the plans as necessary. Analyzing data within this structure allows principals to assess the trajectory of their schools in relation to the goal(s). District officials can support principals in creating documents and talking points for communication with stakeholder groups as a result of these sessions.

Tune Plans in a Principal-PLC*

Horizontal alignment among schools is increased when principals (and their leadership teams) have an opportunity to share their SIPs, analyze one another's plans, provide feedback, and enhance their coherence. Peers serve as thought partners, coaches, or critical friends by asking probing questions that encourage reflection and clarity. Protocols such as the Tuning Protocol (Appendix B.10), facilitated by district-level leaders, allow principals to think deeply about their data metrics, implementation plans, and strategic action steps. Principals then take this collaborative feedback from their peers back to their SIP action teams to refine their work as necessary.

Embrace Continuous Improvement*

School leaders must embrace the reality that an SIP is not a final destination; rather, it is a continuous journey anchoring them to their current and ongoing site needs. Grounding leaders in theories such as Deming's Plan-Do-Study-Act (PDSA) cycle provides a framework for continuously assessing and refining aspects of the SIP (Deming, 1993).

- Plan: Create a plan to address a particular need.
- Do: Implement the plan.
- Study: Analyze the impact of the plan on the identified need.
- Act: Respond to the information by modifying the plan as necessary.

For a graphic detailing the PDSA cycle, see the Continuous Improvement Cycle (Appendix B.11). District staff can set aside time to review SIPs, site data, and modification efforts with school leaders on a quarterly basis to determine what actions are contributing to (or impeding) their successful implementation. This provides an opportunity for adjustments and realignment with site needs.

Criterion 4

Guiding Question: How can we make decisions based on a pursuit of our common goal(s)?

Theory of Action: Principals make roughly 88 billion decisions every day, or so it seems. With each decision, the school should take one step closer toward reaching its agreed-upon goal(s), even in the midst of changing conditions. Using the school's vision and SIP as the basis for decision making may be unpopular and make some people uncomfortable, yet it is essential for ongoing success (Bossidy & Charan, 2002). If the principal compels and partners with constituents to innovate, support, and promote the school's mission and vision, then all decisions will support the pursuit and accomplishment of the common goal(s).

In Figure 3.5, the Principal's Continuum of Self-Reflection describes the depth of thinking related to leadership actions in this criterion. To the right of each stage is the focus behavior for developing reflective capacity within the criterion. Refer to the Reflective Cycle (Figure 2.3, p. 17) and the focused reflective questions (Figure 2.4, p. 22) for more guidance.

FIGURE 3.5

P-CSR: Visionary Criterion 4

UNAWARE STAGE	BUILD AWARENESS	CONSCIOUS STAGE	PLAN INTENTIONALLY	ACTION STAGE	ACCURATELY ASSESS IMPACT	REFINEMENT STAGE	BECOME RESPONSIVE
Makes decisions independent of or contrary to the mission and vision.		Makes decisions that may or may not be aligned with the mission and vision.		Utilizes the school's mission and vision to provide rationale for actions and decisions.		Compels and partners with constituents to innovate, support, and promote the school's mission and vision.	

Pathway One: School Level

Clarify Group Parameters*

Designing school improvement planning efforts, aligning behaviors with agreed-upon goals, and promoting the school's mission and vision require broad-based involvement of all stakeholders. Effective principals recognize this importance and clearly articulate the expected decision-making practices and parameters of each stakeholder group or planning team's authority. They clarify the decision-making expectations (input to principal, consensus, or majority rule) held for each task at the onset of the group's work. This avoids misunderstandings, hurt feelings, a sense of wasted time, or other barriers to achieving the goal(s). (For tips on building consensus, see Appendix B.12.)

It is equally important for the principal to express any nonnegotiables and/or the presence of "veto" power. One word of caution, though: effective principals give thoughtful consideration to the tasks and decision-making process they distribute and rarely have to trump a subgroup's given authority, lest they risk chipping away at the culture they are trying to establish.

Filter Decisions

There are times and events that require principals to make decisions themselves. In the end, after all, it is the principal's signature at the bottom of the form—and that ultimate authority carries a great responsibility. How do principals determine if a request or expenditure will propel the school toward the goal or if it's tangential to the site's ambitions? It stands to reason that if principals must justify their decisions in light of the SIP, then the requesting party (e.g., teacher or stakeholder group) should provide a justification as part of the proposal process.

Many great ideas do not withstand the test of simple filtering questions such as the following: Is this the best course of action to accomplish a certain goal? What other options are there? What are the pros and cons of each? How is this request embedded in the SIP? If this action were published on the Internet, could we confidently address anyone who challenged its merit? By establishing a filtering system that includes questions such as these, principals can usher promising strategies forth while sending others back to the drawing board—without stifling creativity and innovation from staff and stakeholders.

Pathway Two: District Level

Expand Their Toolkits*

Central office administrators and supervisors can enhance a principal's success by learning and practicing the use of varied decision-making processes. This includes understanding types and purpose of decisions, developing clear criteria for making decisions, and evaluating the outcomes of various decisions. When principals have an understanding of decision-making techniques such as the Funneling Consensus Model (Appendix B.13), their effectiveness is increased by soliciting and engaging the opinions of stakeholders regarding decision-making rationale for learning opportunities.

Supervisors can engage their principals in regular discussions to debrief, process, and reflect upon recent decisions. This debriefing process could include an analysis of how intentionally and strategically the principal acted in the decision-making process, and it can examine alternative strategies that may have yielded different (and possibly more successful) results. With this body of knowledge and skills, principals will be more skilled and can pull from a toolkit to apply the appropriate technique to match the task.

Navigate Difficult Situations*

Partnering with constituents provides an opportunity for principals to encounter varied personalities and increases the likelihood of disagreements, arguments, and differences of opinion. When this occurs, the principal must remain above the fray, setting the tone by handling the conflict in a professional, respectful manner. By keeping the conversation aimed toward the intended positive outcomes, focusing on what's best for students, and emphasizing the SIP goals, principals can diffuse many disagreements and channel the energy toward problem solving. Jennings (2007) describes and provides strategies for handling five common types of troublesome meeting participants: the naysayer, the aggressor, the dominator, the attention seeker, and the avoider. We offer some sample approaches for handling each of these difficult roles in Appendix B.14. District staff can use recent incidents or create realistic scenarios to help principals anticipate and adeptly navigate difficult situations before they occur.

Where to Start

Gaining a comprehensive understanding of the principal's role as Visionary is one thing; synthesizing the complex bank of strategies into the nuanced context of a particular school or district is another thing altogether. Before we offer a suggested course of action, let us be clear: it is neither our intent nor our expectation that school or district leaders take the strategies discussed in this chapter as "marching orders," proceeding through the list and checking them off when "complete." Rather, they are options for growing as a visionary leader while simultaneously developing as a reflective practitioner.

In the following section (see Figure 3.6), we have included a self-assessment guide to help provide clarity and direction for your next steps. Though this can be used as a self-directed growth tool, it is preferable to utilize it collaboratively—with peers, colleagues, and supervisors—in order to extract the maximum benefit. For principal supervisors and district officials, this guide can be particularly useful when sitting down with building leaders to set goals, analyze performance, and create a plan to build leadership capacity within the role of Visionary.

Directions for the Self-Assessment Guide

1. Review the stages of the Principal's Continuum of Self-Reflection (P-CSR) along each criterion.
2. Highlight words or phrases and jot down notes regarding your reflective tendencies and professional practice within each criterion.
3. Depending on the stage of the P-CSR at which you believe you are operating, identify the action from the Reflective Cycle that requires your focus.

a. If you are operating in the Unaware stage, your goal is to build awareness.
b. If you are operating in the Conscious stage, your goal is to plan intentionally.
c. If you are operating in the Action stage, your goal is to assess impact.
d. If you are operating in the Refinement stage, your goal is to become responsive.

4. Select a strategy from either Pathway One (school level) or Pathway Two (district level) that will help you address this criterion.
5. After completing this task for all four criteria within the principal's role as Visionary, collaboratively select the one key criterion on which you are ready to focus.
6. Use the Reflective Leadership Planning Template (Appendix A) to create a thorough, robust plan for growing as a visionary leader while simultaneously developing as a reflective practitioner.

FIGURE 3.6
Principal as Visionary Self-Assessment Guide

	UNAWARE STAGE	CONSCIOUS STAGE	ACTION STAGE	REFINEMENT STAGE
CRITERION 1: Articulates, communicates, and leads the collaborative implementation and ongoing revision of the school's mission and vision.	Lacks understanding or development of personal impact on the school's mission and vision.	Understands the mission and vision of the school.	Articulates and communicates the mission and vision of the school.	Initiates and proactively leads the communication, implementation, and ongoing revision of the school's mission, vision, and SIP.

1. Why do you feel this stage is an accurate representation of your thinking about this criterion?

2. Which action from the Reflective Cycle requires your focus in order to grow as a reflective practitioner? (See Figure 2.3 for guidance.)
    Build Awareness   Plan Intentionally   Accurately Assess Progress   Be Responsive

3. Which strategy listed under Criterion 1 might best support your growth as you take action?

	UNAWARE STAGE	CONSCIOUS STAGE	ACTION STAGE	REFINEMENT STAGE
CRITERION 2: Aligns and bases all decisions, practices, policies, and resources (e.g., human capital, time, budgetary, and facilities) on the school's mission and vision.	Allocates resources and engages in practices without alignment to the school's mission and vision.	Addresses situations without overtly connecting the school's data-informed needs to the mission and vision.	Aligns school decisions, practices, and resources with the mission and vision.	Weighs and bases all decisions, practices, and resources to implement and sustain the mission, vision, and SIP.

1. Why do you feel this stage is an accurate representation of your thinking about this criterion?

2. Which action from the Reflective Cycle requires your focus in order to grow as a reflective practitioner? (See Figure 2.3 for guidance.)
    Build Awareness   Plan Intentionally   Accurately Assess Progress   Be Responsive

3. Which strategy listed under Criterion 2 might best support your growth as you take action?

Continued

FIGURE 3.6

Principal as Visionary Self-Assessment Guide (continued)

	UNAWARE STAGE	CONSCIOUS STAGE	ACTION STAGE	REFINEMENT STAGE
CRITERION 3: Promotes the collaborative creation, monitoring, and refinement of short- and long-term school improvement plans.	May or may not access site needs assessment and/or School Improvement Plan.	Takes actions that may or may not take into account the site needs assessment and/or SIP.	Promotes the development and application of SIP based on the site needs assessment.	Collaboratively creates, monitors, and refines the SIP based on needs assessment data points.

1. Why do you feel this stage is an accurate representation of your thinking about this criterion?
2. Which action from the Reflective Cycle requires your focus in order to grow as a reflective practitioner? (See Figure 2.3 for guidance.)
   Build Awareness   Plan Intentionally   Accurately Assess Progress   Be Responsive
3. Which strategy listed under Criterion 3 might best support your growth as you take action?

	UNAWARE STAGE	CONSCIOUS STAGE	ACTION STAGE	REFINEMENT STAGE
CRITERION 4: Compels the district and school community to embrace and work toward the attainment of the shared mission and vision.	Makes decisions independent of or contrary to the mission and vision.	Makes decisions that may or may not be aligned with the mission and vision.	Utilizes the school's mission and vision to provide rationale for actions and decisions.	Compels and partners with constituents to innovate, support, and promote the school's mission and vision.

1. Why do you feel this stage is an accurate representation of your thinking about this criterion?
2. Which action from the Reflective Cycle requires your focus in order to grow as a reflective practitioner? (See Figure 2.3 for guidance.)
   Build Awareness   Plan Intentionally   Accurately Assess Progress   Be Responsive
3. Which strategy listed under Criterion 4 might best support your growth as you take action?

CHAPTER 4
Principal as Instructional Leader

This is not your grandfather's principalship. We're smack dab in the center of the Era of Accountability, which began about 15 years or so ago, and the school principal's responsibility has shifted significantly: from organizational management to instructional leadership. The term *instructional leader* has become ubiquitous, but what does it really mean, in spirit and in practice? In our results-driven culture of schooling, the principal's responsibility and requirement is plain: to demand and develop high-quality learning experiences in every classroom, at every minute, for every child. The principal, so named for the position's original role as "principal teacher," is the gatekeeper for instructional excellence.

There are four criteria within the PLDF for the principal who serves as Instructional Leader. Each is described in greater depth below, and strategies for building leadership capacity within each criterion complete the chapter.

- Criterion 1: Builds collective capacity of the entire staff through the cultivation of a robust Professional Learning Community.
- Criterion 2: Builds individual capacity of the entire staff through differentiated supervision, coaching, feedback, and evaluation practices.
- Criterion 3: Ensures the alignment of rigorous curricula, research-based best practices in instruction, and comprehensive formative and summative assessment approaches.
- Criterion 4: Promotes monitoring systems that use real-time data to inform instruction and intervention at the teacher, team, and school levels.

Criterion 1: Builds collective capacity of the entire staff through the cultivation of a robust Professional Learning Community

The days of closed-door teaching are over. Collaboration is the new norm, and interdependence is the new expectation. The principal's ability to create a school-wide collaborative culture is directly correlated to the amount of success a school experiences—as measured, first and foremost, by indicators of student learning. This culture, often referred to as a Professional Learning Community (PLC), is a proven philosophy that guides meaningful collective capacity-building efforts. Coauthors Hall and Simeral define a PLC as "a collective of educators who always strive to perform at their ultimate potential, working together to learn, grow, and improve the professional practice of teaching in order to maximize student learning" (2008, p. 17).

Explicit in that definition is the shared commitment to learning. In the words of Rick DuFour, an important voice in the PLC movement, "Schools need leadership from principals who focus on advancing student and staff learning" (2002, p. 14). An effective PLC and its team-based structure offer opportunities for teachers to capitalize on one another's strengths, lean on one another for support, pool resources, and share the monumental burden of educating children.

Building and maintaining an effective PLC is more than instituting structural pieces. At its core, the PLC is oriented toward the philosophy of teamwork, prioritizing learning and emphasizing results (DuFour & Eaker, 1998). Though a lone principal could establish a PLC within a single school, savvy district officials know that since it takes a village to raise a child, the entire district and community rallying together—in all the system's schools—will contribute to a stronger, more effective venture. By providing adequate resources, professional development, time to collaborate, and supports, districts can equip schools and principals with the necessary pieces to be successful. PLCs must be nurtured and modeled; the more a district acts as a PLC itself, the more likely its schools will follow suit.

INSTRUCTIONAL LEADERSHIP IN ACTION

Coauthor Phyllis Pajardo, former assistant superintendent in Fairfax County (Virginia) Public Schools, has always been committed to the PLC philosophy and its primary focus: learning. In order to strengthen the learning of the principals she supervised as leaders of PLCs, Pajardo's 28 K–12 schools were structured into three feeder-pattern PLC teams. Working with her principals, she refocused and repurposed their administrative meetings to meet the goals of the PLC approach. No longer would so-called administrivia be allowed. After assessing principals' readiness and implementation, Pajardo recruited them to cofacilitate the "pyramid PLC" meetings, share successes and challenges, examine data, and create common formative assessments.

She met regularly with meeting cofacilitators to build their skills in collaborative leadership, encouraging them to structure their meetings by modeling effective strategies that principals could take back to their schools. By encouraging principals to examine their own practices critically, and by providing the support and tools necessary to engage in this critical work, she created the conditions for those same principals to become more collaborative, interdependent, and capable leaders of the PLC philosophy in their own buildings. According to Pajardo, "Building collective capacity is important because it identifies, recognizes, and celebrates the strengths, talents, and abilities of others."

Criterion 2: Builds individual capacity of the entire staff through differentiated supervision, coaching, feedback, and evaluation practices

As vital as effective teams and the PLC are to school (and district) improvement efforts, individual teacher performance is critical to individual student learning. Since teacher quality is the primary determinant of student success, it stands to reason that principals as instructional leaders tend to the development, growth, and effectiveness of each individual teacher on staff.

In *Results Now*, Mike Schmoker lays the claim that "the single greatest determinant of learning is not socioeconomic factors or funding levels. It is instruction" (2006, p. 7). Therefore, effective principals allocate a significant amount of their time to visiting classrooms, providing actionable feedback to teachers, engaging in deep conversations with staff about planning and instruction, and encouraging regular opportunities to build reflective capacity—going well beyond the minimum requirements of the teacher evaluation process. The principal is the head coach, using all means necessary—professional learning, dialogue, evaluation, data analysis, and more—to promote the ongoing growth and effectiveness of the teaching corps.

INSTRUCTIONAL LEADERSHIP IN ACTION

As the principal of Sheridan Elementary School in Spokane, Washington, coauthor Pete Hall embraced the notion that teacher quality determines student learning outcomes, and he was going to leave nothing to chance. Looking to support his teachers' implementation of best practices in order to maximize student learning, Hall led a comprehensive instructional improvement effort. Starting with an investigation of data-supported instructional strategies, the Sheridan staff gathered their experiences and research to deepen and synthesize their understanding of each best practice. Then, through differentiated coaching and tailored support through a feedback-rich walkthrough process, Hall guided staff as they refined their instructional practices.

He held sacred the time during which students and teachers were engaged in learning and teaching experiences in the classroom. Nothing trumped those "precious moments," as he called them, and he visited classrooms to gauge progress, provide feedback, and "talk teaching" with his teachers every day. Strategic follow-through was crucial to ensure that teachers were taking deliberate action and student learning was indeed increasing (Hall & Simeral, 2008). This model led to several academic achievement awards for the Sheridan campus. Said one teacher upon Hall's departure, "I'm ten times the teacher I was before you got here."

How do district leaders ensure that their principals—both current and future—are involved in the instructional components of their schools? And how can principal supervisors build the capacity of their principals to serve as effective Instructional Leaders? A districtwide support system for leadership in schools must be systemic, be results driven, build collective responsibility, and include some quality assurance aspects. Like many things, district officials must also practice what they preach by engaging in professional learning opportunities that encourage professional collaboration, include in-depth investigation of instructional strategies, and involve job-embedded application and feedback about leadership practices (City, Elmore, Fiarman, & Teitel, 2009; Marzano et al., 2005). It is also essential for districts to establish meaningful teacher and principal evaluation systems that support ongoing professional learning (Danielson, 2007; Stronge, Xu, Leeper, & Tonneson, 2013).

Criterion 3: Ensures the alignment of rigorous curricula, research-based best practices in instruction, and comprehensive formative and summative assessment approaches

Curriculum, instruction, and assessment—often known as the CIA of education—is truly the central source of intelligence in our education agency. Effective principals have a firm grasp of all three. They understand them as individual elements and as interrelated components of a cohesive educational plan. According to research, a principal's knowledge of CIA had the strongest relationship with second-order (i.e., deep, lasting) change (Marzano et al., 2005).

Do principals have to know everything about every course in every subject in every grade level? That might be asking a bit much, though it's essential for principals to know enough to know what questions to ask. Success with CIA is a complex exercise in connecting the dots among the three pieces. Principals must first embrace the content, course, or grade standards and the curriculum, which is the blueprint for achieving the desired student performance (Wiggins & McTighe, 2005). A thorough knowledge of effective instructional practices (e.g., Dean, Hubbell, Pitler, & Stone, 2012; Goodwin & Hubbell, 2013; Hattie, 2009), including differentiated instruction (Tomlinson, 2014), the gradual release of responsibility model (Fisher & Frey, 2014), and a common instructional framework (e.g., Danielson, 2007), shape a principal's ability to shepherd both learning and teaching. Finally, developing linked formative and summative assessment practices, and distinguishing between the two depending on the purpose, completes the leader's role in connecting the CIA dots (Moss & Brookhart, 2009; Popham, 2008).

District officials can support school leaders by helping them unpack standards, analyze curriculum, evaluate instructional techniques, and implement assessment strategies that are aligned in the CIA triangle. There is bountiful research (see the preceding paragraph for a sampling of the reams of studies on instructional "best practices") that indicates we already know what we need to know in order to positively affect learning for all students. According to McREL CEO Bryan Goodwin, "One of the most powerful things school systems can do to change the odds for all students is simply doing *well* what they already know they must do" (2011, p. 134). The district's responsibility is to provide opportunities for its current and future leaders to learn, implement, assess, and refine their agreed-upon menu of best practices.

INSTRUCTIONAL LEADERSHIP IN ACTION

While serving as the assistant superintendent of learning and teaching (a position she renamed in order to prioritize learning) in the Renton (Washington) Public Schools, Dr. Tammy Campbell insisted that every initiative, system, and process was aligned toward the ultimate goal: increased student learning for every child. This meant that she pulled out all the stops to ensure that the district fully supported principals as instructional leaders. By renaming the principal supervisors "area instructional chiefs" and repurposing those positions to observe principal practice, coach, collaborate, and consult with principals for the purpose of improving student learning, Campbell created the conditions for principals to effectively supply instructional leadership.

The area instructional chiefs, former successful principals with deep knowledge of effective instruction themselves, brought a lens of cultural competency and a focus on students and student results, and they were willing to engage in the courageous act of pushing practice. Their success is measured by principals' success, which is in turn measured by student success. As a result, rather than having isolated buildings thriving and others struggling, the district is engaged in a systemwide effort of continuous improvement.

Criterion 4: Promotes monitoring systems that use real-time data to inform instruction and intervention at the teacher, team, and school levels

Historically, those in the profession of education have had their data dumped upon them—usually late, in an undecipherable format, and on measures the receivers were unaware of. In recent years, experts have shared ways to use data in a meaningful way, and it is now commonplace to hear principals, teachers, and district officials discussing how to use data to improve teaching and learning. If only it were that simple. Effective instructional leaders know that they have access to terabytes of various student achievement data, and the key is to intentionally filter the voluminous files, select those that measure specific learning outcomes, and analyze them thoughtfully.

Principals lead their teams in investigation and data examinations, using systematic processes (Bernhardt, 2009; Venables, 2014) or protocols (Easton, 2009) to make sense of the data and to plot a course of action as a result. Within the structure of the PLC (see Criterion 1, earlier), data-savvy teams create common formative assessments and analyze their results immediately, providing a better opportunity for teachers to enact meaningful interventions. Principals, as instructional leaders, provide the structure, oversight, and support to make this happen.

INSTRUCTIONAL LEADERSHIP IN ACTION

Student data discourse dominated the airwaves at The Frank Sansivieri Intermediate School, a 6–8 public school in New York, under the leadership of principal Patricia Reynolds. Convinced that every teacher action must be decisive, intentional, and immediate, Reynolds led the staff to create a system in which teachers provided on-time support within lessons in their own classrooms rather than wait for an after-school program or a specialist to pull struggling students out for interventions. Using collaboratively built formative assessments, exit tickets, and other tools, teachers responded to student needs by hosting in-lesson mini-conferences. Reynolds supported teachers' efforts by leading data-driven dialogues with teams, reviewing teachers' assessment notebooks, and conferencing with teachers to analyze exit tickets. "We knew what student performance should look like," Reynolds says. "And that made it easy to spot student success and failure." These practices guided the planning for instructional emphases and professional learning for staff as well. Under her watch, the 1,600-student, diverse, urban school made staggering academic gains and propelled itself into "Good Standing" under state accountability measures.

To a larger degree, school district officials provide the same structures, oversights, and supports to help principals lead their work with data at the school level. By providing access to meaningful, relevant data in a timely fashion—and by eliminating extraneous assessments that serve no useful purpose—district leaders can ensure that principals and leadership teams streamline their efforts toward a beneficial goal. Often, districts must coordinate a systematic approach to selecting data, practice analyzing it for trends and outliers, and reinforce the helpfulness of regular data inquiry cycles (Boudett et al., 2005). The more a school district operates like a PLC itself, the more the data live in the dialogue and become embedded in the work of the leaders.

Growing as an Instructional Leader: Strategies for Reflective Growth

In the following sections, we offer several strategies for building principals' leadership capacity within this role. Each provides the opportunity for the principal (Pathway One) and the district-level supervisors (Pathway Two) to clarify the work and streamline all efforts toward the long-term outcome: develop and refine reflective practices while simultaneously augmenting expertise in these criteria. Simply put, we're aiming for principals to operate in the Refinement stage as instructional leaders.

The strategies we offer in Figure 4.1 are but a sampling of the many avenues to approach growth within each criterion. The strategies we have selected deliver high-leverage, universal results, and many of them include tools, templates, protocols, and forms you can find in Appendix B and online at www.ascd.org/ASCD/pdf/books/TPI2016.pdf. It is our intent to provide immediately actionable, easily implemented strategies that bridge the gap between research and application. Strategies with a support resource in Appendix B are marked with an asterisk (*).

With a thorough understanding of the role and criteria that contribute to effective instructional leadership within the role of an instructional leader, a good place to begin is with an honest self-assessment. Reflect on each criterion as a separate piece of your leadership puzzle. Within each criterion, we have added a brief self-assessment

FIGURE 4.1

Principal as Instructional Leader Strategy Schematic

	CRITERION 1: Builds collective capacity of the entire staff through the cultivation of a robust Professional Learning Community.	CRITERION 2: Builds individual capacity of the entire staff through differentiated supervision, coaching, feedback, and evaluation practices.	CRITERION 3: Ensures the alignment of rigorous curricula, research-based best practices in instruction, and comprehensive formative and summative assessment approaches.	CRITERION 4: Promotes monitoring systems that use real-time data to inform instruction and intervention at the teacher, team, and school levels.
PATHWAY ONE: SCHOOL LEVEL	• Distribute Leadership Within PLCs • Create and Protect Time • Drive PLCs with Protocols*	• Utilize a Performance-Based Supervision and Evaluation Model* • Provide Feedback That Feeds Forward*	• Build an Agreed-upon Definition of Best Practices* • Facilitate Instructional Rounds* • Create Peer Coaching Triad Teams*	• Employ Student Work Protocols* • Adopt a Data Action Model*
PATHWAY TWO: DISTRICT LEVEL	• Develop a Results-Based Professional Learning Community* • Create Connected Learning Communities	• Create a Community of Critical Friends* • Build upon Strengths	• Synthesize District Benchmark Assessments • Facilitate School-to-School Observations*	• Set Data Expectations • Engage Principals in Data-Driven Dialogues*

Note: Strategies with an asterisk (*) include a tool/template/protocol/form in Appendix B.

guide to facilitate leaders' exploration of their current thinking and technical proficiency. In the Reflective Leadership Planning Template (found in Appendix A and downloadable at www.ascd.org/ASCD/pdf/books/TPI2016.pdf), we suggest that principals (or assistant principals or aspiring principals) sit down with their supervisors/mentors/coaches and collaboratively record a narrative of their own current reality, including where they currently operate on the Principal's Continuum of Self-Reflection.

After scrutinizing the sample strategies that follow and collaboratively brainstorming additional strategies (with colleagues, supervisors, and others in your professional learning network), use the Reflective Leadership Planning Template to document the powerful steps you will take to develop your (or your principal's) growth as a reflective instructional leader. There is great strength in the dialogue, collaboration, and partnership in this goal-setting endeavor; utilize the resources at your disposal to create and refine a clear, focused, reflection-oriented plan.

Criterion 1

Guiding Question: How can we learn together, grow together, and work together to support student and adult learning?

Theory of Action: The expression "It takes a village to raise a child" has never been more spot-on than it is right now in education. When professional educators work together as a collaborative team focused on student learning outcomes, the result is an increase in student achievement and stronger professional practice (Caine & Caine, 2010). If the principal builds the collective capacity of the entire staff through the cultivation of a robust and equitable student-focused PLC, then student learning will increase in a continuous cycle of improvement.

In Figure 4.2, the Principal's Continuum of Self-Reflection describes the depth of thinking related to leadership actions in this criterion. To the right of each stage is the focus behavior for developing reflective capacity within the criterion. Refer to the Reflective Cycle (Figure 2.3, p. 17) and the focused reflective questions (Figure 2.4, p. 22) for more guidance.

FIGURE 4.2

P-CSR: *Instructional Leader Criterion 1*

UNAWARE STAGE	BUILD AWARENESS	CONSCIOUS STAGE	PLAN INTENTIONALLY	ACTION STAGE	ACCURATELY ASSESS IMPACT	REFINEMENT STAGE	BECOME RESPONSIVE
Has not enacted steps toward developing a PLC.		Organizes school staff with some elements of PLC present.		Facilitates the implementation of the structural elements of a PLC.		Builds collective capacity of entire staff through the cultivation of a robust and equitable student focused PLC.	

Pathway One: School Level

Distribute Leadership within PLCs

A successful Professional Learning Community is characterized in part by a wide distribution of leadership throughout the organization. In that vein, it is essential for effective principals to grow strong teacher leaders by recruiting and accepting volunteers. To best leverage classroom expertise and leadership roles, principals can create structures that will support their success. First, start by identifying potential leaders, noting that highly effective in the classroom doesn't always mean highly effective in leadership roles.

Look for qualities, characteristics, and evidence of reflective tendencies. Strong teacher leaders engage in reflection often and deeply about both their practice and their role as practitioners. After identifying teacher leaders, conduct an assessment of their knowledge, skills, and dispositions regarding leadership and facilitation skills. When ready, invite them to facilitate team meetings within the PLC structure, host a lab classroom, organize an action research project, or collaborate on the SIP. Provide opportunities for them to lead professional development, encourage their pursuit of innovative ideas, and support them as a network of leaders as you build an environment of collegiality, trust, and respect. Teacher leaders shape the culture of their school, improve student learning, and influence instructional practice among their peers. They are one of the principal's most valuable resources.

Create and Protect Time

Finding time for teams to meet can be one of the greatest challenges for a principal who is implementing Professional Learning Communities, yet this is one of the highest-leverage strategies for principals who want to cultivate robust PLCs. Start with the master daily schedule and build in common planning opportunities for collaborative teams. In elementary schools, "blocking" specials in consecutive periods can extend teams' collaborative meeting time. At the secondary level, teaming and incorporating team time or intervention blocks can free teachers to meet collaboratively. Utilize quarterly substitutes to provide additional collaboration opportunities. Free up time for teams to meet by relieving teachers from routine duties and cutting back on unnecessary obligations. Make better use of time by transforming faculty meetings into collective learning opportunities, and focus dialogue on student success, data analysis, and professional learning rather than on management and logistical issues. How time is used in a school says a lot about that school's purpose and priorities—and making time for collaboration enables staff to spend this fleeting resource on the work that will most directly and positively affect student learning.

Drive PLCs with Protocols*

Protocols are an agreed-upon set of guidelines for conversation—a structured code of behavior that groups adhere to when discussing and exploring ideas, examining student work, and reflecting on teacher pedagogy. They come in many different shapes and sizes, and part of the adventure of a PLC is the opportunity to discover which protocol works best for which team. In her book *Protocols for Professional Learning*, Lois Brown Easton (2009) details 16 different protocols that can be used to facilitate discussion in a variety of formats for a variety of purposes. Building leaders should become familiar with the protocols and model their everyday use in the meetings they hold.

When ready, introduce several to the staff, providing teams with an opportunity to choose which to use. Purpose for the protocols should be explicitly connected to a school's mission, vision, and driving values, and principals should elicit feedback from groups after their use. The effective practice of protocols builds the capacity of team members and maintains a focus on student learning throughout the PLC. We have included several of Easton's protocols, either in their original or modified versions, in Appendices B.3, B.10, and B.18.

Pathway Two: District Level

Develop a Results-Based Professional Learning Community*

A district must have methods in place to ensure that all schools are engaging in the PLC process, and that these processes are positively affecting student achievement. There are two steps to setting this up. First, identify established district priorities and develop a set of behaviors and practices that would be evident in a principal's practice in supporting the PLC work within a school building. Collaboratively, set goals based on the principal's current level of thinking on the Principal's Continuum of Self-Reflection (P-CSR) related to these priorities. This serves to build collective responsibility and bring alignment from the district level to the school and classroom level. Second, as supervisors and coaches work with individual principals, feedback should target growth along the P-CSR as each principal works toward building effective school-based PLCs. Use the tool provided in Appendix B.15 to guide your work.

Create Connected Learning Communities

As modern technology has brought educators around the world closer to one another, the opportunity to learn and collaborate with colleagues is often more easily found in the global arena than it is in one's own district and school. A connected learning community provides both teachers and principals with the opportunity to link their individual learning through social media and online communities with school and district-level learning and collaboration. By integrating both local and global learning, a district can transform its professional development into a powerful professional learning system and thereby build capacity within districtwide PLCs. Start by increasing awareness of and model participation in online learning opportunities. From there, incentivize and reward participation in online learning by offering formal micro-credentials, recertification hours, or in-service credits. Use technology to support instructional teams, allowing them to work together across distances and share results globally. To bring this practice closer to home, provide face-to-face, blended, and online professional development opportunities at the district level. A connected learning community has the power to take school-level PLCs to the next level.

Criterion 2

Guiding Question: How can we maximize the instructional skill and reflective capacity of each individual teacher on staff?

Theory of Action: Classroom instruction is the primary determinant of student success. Affecting that single variable will have the greatest cumulative effect on student learning (Schmoker, 2006). If a principal builds individual and collective capacity of the entire staff through differentiated supervision, coaching, and evaluation processes, then classroom instruction will improve and lead to increased student learning.

In Figure 4.3, the Principal's Continuum of Self-Reflection describes the depth of thinking related to leadership actions in this criterion. To the right of each stage is the focus behavior for developing reflective capacity within the criterion. Refer to the Reflective Cycle (Figure 2.3, p. 17) and the focused reflective questions (Figure 2.4, p. 22) for more guidance.

FIGURE 4.3

P-CSR: Instructional Leader Criterion 2

UNAWARE STAGE	BUILD AWARENESS	CONSCIOUS STAGE	PLAN INTENTIONALLY	ACTION STAGE	ACCURATELY ASSESS IMPACT	REFINEMENT STAGE	BECOME RESPONSIVE
Adheres to the formal observation process and does not go beyond that.		Completes the formal evaluation process and may or may not pursue further monitoring of instruction.		Supervises and monitors instruction, providing feedback to teachers.		Builds individual and collective capacity of entire staff through differentiated supervision, coaching, and evaluation practices.	

Pathway One: School Level

Utilize a Performance-Based Supervision and Evaluation Model*

When principals want to make sure their teachers' emphasis resides on student learning and connected teacher practice, the adopted supervision and evaluation model can provide a conduit for this practice. In this strategy, the principal guides a teacher to choose current, relevant student assessment data that will be the focus of reflection and determines agenda topics for supervisory check-ins. By using this model, the authors of *Supervision for Learning* state, "the capacity for using student data analytically to improve teaching and learning empowers the whole of the teachers' work . . . and the potential rewards are great: demonstrated professional competence and growth that result in improved student learning and greater organizational capacity for change" (Aseltine, Faryniarz, & Rigazio-DiGilio, 2006).

Furthermore, this enables both the teacher and the evaluator to identify the cause-and-effect relationship between particular instructional strategies and student learning outcomes rather than look solely at teacher inputs. Using the template provided in Appendix B.16, create an individual professional development plan together with the teacher, outlining how his or her colleagues might support growth, detailing resources available, and determining the targeted focus for walkthroughs, feedback, and discussions about teaching and learning.

Provide Feedback That Feeds Forward*

Feedback that will propel teachers forward forms and shapes the thinking of classroom teachers. It draws out their best performance and provides suggestions for improvement. In order for feedback to be effective, it must follow four criteria: it must be timely, specific, understandable, and allow the teacher to act in a forward way by refining, revising, retrying, or practicing (Wiggins, 1998). In *Building Teachers' Capacity for Success* (Hall & Simeral, 2008), principals can find examples of the specific language that deepens teachers' reflective processes and matches their current stage on the Continuum of Self-Reflection. Such feedback stems launch productive principal-teacher dialogue, spur deeper reflections, and provide actionable feedback. After determining a teacher's reflective standing on the teacher version of the Continuum of Self-Reflection, use the feedback guide provided in Appendix B.17 to speak the right language at the right time to the right teacher. This is feedback that feeds forward.

Pathway Two: District Level

Create a Community of Critical Friends*

A critical friends network is a group of professionals (leaders, in this case) who come together to wrestle with specific problems of practice, spending time to collaboratively engage in problem-solving processes. The critical friends challenge one another, ask probing questions, deliver straightforward feedback, diversify the collective leadership repertoire, and expand one another's thinking. To create such a network, bring together four to six principals from feeder schools led by a coach or supervisor. Develop a recurring meeting schedule and familiarize group members with the Consultancy Protocol (provided in Appendix B.18), which will help them discuss their problems of practice. As principals surface particular concerns, arrange the agenda to include the most pressing items first. As group members become more familiar with the protocol, the leaders grow as a collaborative, interdependent team of professional learners.

Build upon Strengths

Building individual capacity and differentiating supervision for principals within a district starts with a supervisor's relationship with each principal and the knowledge of that principal's strengths and talents.

Beginning with strengths helps principals, too: "The key to human development is building on who you already are" (Rath, 2007, p. 8). Ask each principal to complete a self-assessment in order to build understanding of skills, dispositions, and strengths. A simple approach would be to convert the district's principal evaluation standards into a self-assessment tool and use it to guide an in-depth conversation about each principal's beliefs, areas of confidence, areas of need, and reflective state of mind. Once the strengths assessment is complete, use it to inform your supervisory role. Have the principal set goals that can be enhanced based on his or her strengths. Utilize the principal's strengths to coach through various situations and provide feedback and an opportunity to engage in deep reflection. The use of a strengths assessment not only builds our awareness of the adults with whom we work but also allows us to be intentional in our supervisory roles and assists in the development of professional growth plans.

Criterion 3

Guiding Question: How can we make sure that curriculum, instruction, and assessment practices are coordinated and aligned to support student learning?

Theory of Action: Curriculum, instruction, and assessment (CIA) provide the backbone of powerful learning experiences for students. When aligned, each informs the other and ultimately supports an environment in which all efforts are focused on student learning (Wiggins & McTighe, 2005). If the principal assures the alignment of curriculum, instruction, and assessment that meet all students' needs, then all students have a greater likelihood of meeting their learning goals.

In Figure 4.4, the Principal's Continuum of Self-Reflection describes the depth of thinking related to leadership actions in this criterion. To the right of each stage is the focus behavior for developing reflective capacity within the criterion. Refer to the Reflective Cycle (Figure 2.3, p. 17) and the focused reflective questions (Figure 2.4, p. 22) for more guidance.

FIGURE 4.4

P-CSR: Instructional Leader Criterion 3

UNAWARE STAGE	BUILD AWARENESS	CONSCIOUS STAGE	PLAN INTENTIONALLY	ACTION STAGE	ACCURATELY ASSESS IMPACT	REFINEMENT STAGE	BECOME RESPONSIVE
Maintains status quo regarding curriculum, instruction, and assessment.		Takes steps to update curriculum, instruction, and assessment practices.		Coordinates curriculum, instruction, and assessment practices.		Assures the alignment of curriculum, instruction, and assessment that meets all students' needs.	

Pathway One: School Level

Build an Agreed-upon Definition of Best Practices*

Alignment of schoolwide CIA starts with building a common understanding of research-supported, high-leverage strategies. Lead staff in an exploration of the research, the district's adopted framework for instructional practice, and the skills necessary for students to master the content and grade-level curriculum. Blend that research with current staff members' experience and expertise, identifying what it would look and sound like if each teaching and assessment strategy were implemented effectively. As staff brainstorm and cite examples, use the protocol included in Appendix B.19 to refine their thinking and arrive at a consensus. The result is a clear, shared understanding of particular CIA strategies (and the specific application of them) that the staff, as a whole, agrees to learn about, implement, and refine. From the principal's perspective, these become nonnegotiable expectations for all staff, and they provide clear look-fors, guidance for professional learning, context for feedback, and content for coaching conversations throughout the building.

Facilitate Instructional Rounds*

Instructional Rounds is a powerful strategy any school or district can utilize to grow the instructional capacity of its teachers and foster a culture of collaboration. The primary purpose is to provide an opportunity for teachers to observe others and compare their instructional practice with those whom they observe. The focus of this strategy ultimately rests on the observers and centers on how each observer will change his or her practice as a result of observing others. To get started, identify a teacher who is highly effective at implementing an identified instructional practice, and arrange for a small group of three to five teachers to visit the classroom for 15–20 minutes. Encourage teachers to focus on the identified strategy while watching for additional strategies that might resonate with them as individuals. After the visit, debrief the process with the group of observing teachers and ask them to identify one instructional practice they will continue to use because they saw it employed effectively during the observation, one instructional practice they will work to refine because of what they saw, and one instructional practice they don't currently use but will try because they observed another teacher's success with it. We have included a handy outline to provide more detail about this process in Appendix B.20.

Create Peer Coaching Triad Teams*

Peer coaching takes instructional rounds to the next level, asking teachers to step into the role of coach and offer focused feedback around a problem of practice to a "coachee" who is a willing participant in the venture. In Triad Team form, a third person enters the picture as an observer, participating in the observation with the coach and bringing closure to the observation experience by facilitating reflective dialogue around the roles each played: coach, coachee, and observer. The principal can deliberately select the members of the team and partner groups of three by content, grade level, experience, learning profile, or some other criteria. Once created, the principal delivers expectations and procedures for the team. Focusing on a schoolwide (or otherwise common) problem of practice, members of the team will rotate through each of the three roles once per quarter or semester (determined by the principal). After a 15- to 20-minute observation in the coachee's classroom, the team will meet to debrief using the Triad Protocol (found in Appendix B.3). As team members rotate through the roles of the Triad Team, they will develop reflective habits and refine their instructional practice.

Pathway Two: District Level

Synthesize District Benchmark Assessments

Central office staff should be able to articulate the connections between multiple adopted initiatives within a district. To maintain vertical alignment throughout the system, principal supervisors can help principals see those connections and lead with that interrelatedness in mind. As schools implement their aligned goals, principals can collect artifacts and evidence of school progress that directly affects district goals. By creating, implementing, revising, and analyzing periodic benchmark assessments of student learning, district leaders, school leaders, and classroom teachers can measure the students' growth toward agreed-upon high-priority standards. Coupling these metrics with classroom observations and anecdotal notes allows leaders to analyze the alignment of CIA practices. District leaders guide the investigation and dialogue about the use of formative assessment tools for various purposes, helping identify strengths, rectify inconsistencies, and build system cohesiveness.

Facilitate School-to-School Observations*

To learn more about high-leverage CIA practices, district staff can identify model schools that have designed, delivered, aligned, and evaluated best practices that resulted in student and staff success. District officials can arrange visitations, during which teams of educators (including a principal, an instructional lead, and several teachers) can observe key strategies in action. During each school visit, the visiting school can use the tool provided in Appendix B.21 to hone their focus, guide their observations, and direct their discussion. As an enriching part of the process, staff from model schools can share the details of their journey by highlighting specific steps taken to implement and institutionalize certain practices, processes, and protocols. In addition to synthesizing the work of the professionals across the system, this strategy creates the opportunity for new and powerful learning partnerships to form between schools.

Criterion 4

Guiding Question: How can we use data to inform our instruction and intervention efforts?

Theory of Action: Education has become a field with data as plentiful as dandelions. It is up to leaders and practitioners to make sure that their ability to access and analyze data is useful to inform instruction and intervention efforts (Boudett et al., 2005). If the principal promotes monitoring systems that utilize real-time data to inform teams' and teachers' instruction and intervention decisions, then all students will have access to appropriate and rigorous learning opportunities.

In Figure 4.5, the Principal's Continuum of Self-Reflection describes the depth of thinking related to leadership actions in this criterion. To the right of each stage is the focus behavior for developing reflective capacity within the criterion. Refer to the Reflective Cycle (Figure 2.3, p. 17) and the focused reflective questions (Figure 2.4, p. 22) for more guidance.

FIGURE 4.5

P-CSR: *Instructional Leader Criterion 4*

UNAWARE STAGE	BUILD AWARENESS	CONSCIOUS STAGE	PLAN INTENTIONALLY	ACTION STAGE	ACCURATELY ASSESS IMPACT	REFINEMENT STAGE	BECOME RESPONSIVE
Does not understand, access, or use available data.		Collects data and may or may not use it to update action plans.		Analyzes data to create and refine action plans.		Promotes monitoring systems that utilize real-time data to inform teams' and teachers' instruction and intervention decisions.	

Pathway One: School Level

Employ Student Work Protocols*

Principals can ensure that teachers and teams are making instructional and intervention decisions based on student needs by employing the widespread use of protocols. When colleagues follow a protocol (an agreed-upon set of directions for engaging in professional dialogue), the result is often a discussion rife with rich conversation, innovative thinking, and incredible focus. The Tuning Protocol (found in Appendix B.10) provides guidelines for examining student work in order to make instructional and intervention decisions. One teacher begins by setting the context of a particular teaching or learning event and shares samples of student work. That teacher's colleagues then engage in a structured set of questions and conversations, ideally deepening the presenting teacher's understanding, revealing a new perspective, or offering strategies for moving forward. For principals to enact this protocol, it is simply a matter of following the guide and carefully debriefing the process afterward. This follow-up is a critical step in surfacing concerns and streamlining the team's work as teachers strive to support one another.

Adopt a Data Action Model*

To systematically inform teaching practices, schools must embrace a long-range cycle of data inquiry that guides instructional and intervention decision making. A Data Action Model is a teacher-friendly, systematic process for reviewing and responding to data in multiple-week cycles. This model is for schoolwide use—principals roll it out after establishing an environment in which formative assessment data has become a valuable commodity. The cycle, by Daniel Venables (2014) and outlined in Appendix B.22, involves a series of data-oriented team meetings during which teacher teams have very clear directions for each of five collaborative sessions: asking key questions, triangulating data, identifying goals, planning for action, and (after an implementation period) analyzing results. When principals lead the charge by setting expectations, participating in data meetings, and following through with teams to celebrate and refine their work, the professional environment shifts to become more data savvy, eventually helping teachers translate data into practice. With experience and expertise, teams embrace the fluidity of this model, focusing on goals and student outcomes through continuous improvement.

Pathway Two: District Level

Set Data Expectations

Supervisors and central office staff can support the ongoing development of principals by setting expectations on the types of data collection expected of leaders. Once the vision is set, the SIP (and the equivalent DIP) is in place, and the key outcomes are defined, district officials can outline the type of data—and even the specific metrics that gauge success of certain initiatives and goals—that are required of their principals. By clarifying what information is expected, principal supervisors can guide principals in the selection of sources for student achievement data, teacher perception data, climate surveys, community feedback, and observational data. This promotes a standard for data awareness and data literacy across the system's leaders.

Engage Principals in Data-Driven Dialogues*

Once the data are collected, district officials can follow up by hosting district-level data-driven dialogues that engage principals in rigorous analysis of their own (and their colleagues') school-level data. To begin, principals need to be provided with timely data periodically throughout the year. These data should highlight the changes and challenges occurring in relationships between the district and school-aligned goals, such as benchmark assessments that schools administer to gauge student learning for a particular set of academic standards. Supervisors and coaches provide ongoing support through focused conversations and actionable problem solving based on data analysis, using the protocol available in Appendix B.6. In addition, this strategy serves to model a data-driven dialogue structure that principals can replicate in their buildings.

Where to Start

Gaining a comprehensive understanding of the principal's role as instructional leader is one thing; synthesizing the complex bank of strategies into the nuanced context of a particular school or district is another thing altogether. Before we offer a suggested course of action, let us be clear: it is neither our intent nor our expectation that school or district leaders take the strategies discussed in this chapter as "marching orders," proceeding through the list and checking them off when "complete." Rather, they are options for growing as an instructional leader while simultaneously developing as a reflective practitioner.

In the following section (see Figure 4.6), we have included a self-assessment guide to help provide clarity and direction for your next steps. Though this can be used as a self-directed growth tool, it is preferable to utilize it collaboratively—with peers, colleagues, and supervisors—in order to extract the maximum benefit. For principal supervisors and district officials, this guide can be particularly useful when sitting down with building leaders to set goals, analyze performance, and create a plan to build leadership capacity within the role of Instructional Leader.

Directions for the Self-Assessment Guide

1. Review the stages of the Principal's Continuum of Self-Reflection (P-CSR) along each criterion.
2. Highlight words or phrases and jot down notes regarding your reflective tendencies and professional practice within each criterion.
3. Depending on the stage of the P-CSR at which you believe you are operating, identify the action from the Reflective Cycle that requires your focus.
   a. If you are operating in the Unaware stage, your goal is to build awareness.
   b. If you are operating in the Conscious stage, your goal is to plan intentionally.

    c.   If you are operating in the Action stage, your goal is to assess impact.

    d.   If you are operating in the Refinement stage, your goal is to become responsive.

4. Select a strategy from either Pathway One (school level) or Pathway Two (district level) that will help you address this criterion.

5. After completing this task for all four criteria within the principal's role as Instructional Leader, collaboratively select the one key criterion on which you are ready to focus.

6. Use the Reflective Leadership Planning Template (Appendix A) to create a thorough, robust plan for growing as an instructional leader while simultaneously developing as a reflective practitioner.

FIGURE 4.6

Principal as Instructional Leader Self-Assessment Guide

	UNAWARE STAGE	CONSCIOUS STAGE	ACTION STAGE	REFINEMENT STAGE
CRITERION 1: Builds collective capacity of the entire staff through the cultivation of a robust Professional Learning Community (PLC).	Has not enacted steps toward developing a PLC.	Organizes school staff with some elements of PLC present.	Facilitates the implementation of the structural elements of a PLC.	Builds collective capacity of entire staff through the cultivation of a robust and equitable student-focused PLC.

1. Why do you feel this stage is an accurate representation of your thinking about this criterion?

2. Which action from the Reflective Cycle requires your focus in order to grow as a reflective practitioner? (See Figure 2.3 for guidance.)
   Build Awareness   Plan Intentionally   Accurately Assess Progress   Be Responsive

3. Which strategy listed under Criterion 1 might best support your growth as you take action?

	UNAWARE STAGE	CONSCIOUS STAGE	ACTION STAGE	REFINEMENT STAGE
CRITERION 2: Builds individual capacity of the entire staff through differentiated supervision, coaching, feedback, and evaluation practices.	Adheres to the formal observation process and does not go beyond that.	Completes the formal evaluation process and may or may not pursue further monitoring of instruction.	Supervises and monitors instruction, providing feedback to teachers.	Builds individual and collective capacity of entire staff through differentiated supervision, coaching, and evaluation practices.

1. Why do you feel this stage is an accurate representation of your thinking about this criterion?

2. Which action from the Reflective Cycle requires your focus in order to grow as a reflective practitioner? (See Figure 2.3 for guidance.)
   Build Awareness   Plan Intentionally   Accurately Assess Progress   Be Responsive

3. Which strategy listed under Criterion 2 might best support your growth as you take action?

Continued

FIGURE 4.6

Principal as Instructional Leader Self-Assessment Guide (continued)

	UNAWARE STAGE	CONSCIOUS STAGE	ACTION STAGE	REFINEMENT STAGE
CRITERION 3: Ensures the alignment of rigorous curricula, research-based best practices in instruction, and comprehensive formative and summative assessment approaches.	Maintains status quo regarding curriculum, instruction, and assessment.	Takes steps to update curriculum, instruction, and assessment practices.	Coordinates curriculum, instruction, and assessment practices.	Assures the alignment of curriculum, instruction, and assessment that meet all students' needs.

1. Why do you feel this stage is an accurate representation of your thinking about this criterion?
2. Which action from the Reflective Cycle requires your focus in order to grow as a reflective practitioner? (See Figure 2.3 for guidance.)
   Build Awareness   Plan Intentionally   Accurately Assess Progress   Be Responsive
3. Which strategy listed under Criterion 3 might best support your growth as you take action?

	UNAWARE STAGE	CONSCIOUS STAGE	ACTION STAGE	REFINEMENT STAGE
CRITERION 4: Promotes monitoring systems that use real-time data to inform instruction and intervention at the teacher, team, and school levels.	Does not understand, access, or use available data.	Collects data and may or may not use it to update action plans.	Analyzes data to create and refine action plans.	Promotes monitoring systems that utilize real-time data to inform teams' and teachers' instruction and intervention decisions.

1. Why do you feel this stage is an accurate representation of your thinking about this criterion?
2. Which action from the Reflective Cycle requires your focus in order to grow as a reflective practitioner? (See Figure 2.3 for guidance.)
   Build Awareness   Plan Intentionally   Accurately Assess Progress   Be Responsive
3. Which strategy listed under Criterion 4 might best support your growth as you take action?

CHAPTER 5
Principal as Engager

The principal is the figurehead of the school. As the visible spokesperson for the entire school community, the principal serves as the ultimate role model—displaying what is important, what is nonnegotiable, and the expectations for conduct and focus. In order to build cohesiveness toward the common vision, and since we cannot *make* anyone do anything, leaders must serve as engagers. Heavy-handed leadership techniques have run their course. Daniel Pink's research on motivation is clear: sticks and carrots do not work. What does? Autonomy, mastery, and purpose (Pink, 2009). By working relentlessly to emphasize common values, principals can subtly engage and influence the entire school community to achieve synergy.

There are five criteria within the PLDF for the principal who serves as Engager. Each is described in greater depth below, and strategies for building leadership capacity within each criterion complete the chapter.

- Criterion 1: Maintains an unwavering priority of establishing and fostering an environment that tends to the Whole Child: healthy, safe, engaged, supported, and challenged.
- Criterion 2: Creates and cultivates partnerships within the parent, district, business, political, and greater community spheres to support the achievement of the school's mission and vision.
- Criterion 3: Drives and navigates positive change by assessing, analyzing, and anticipating emerging trends and implementing change-savvy techniques with staff and the school community.
- Criterion 4: Safeguards community values, ethics, and equitable practices, advocating for all children and displaying an appreciation for diversity.
- Criterion 5: Develops policies and practices that cultivate staff as reflective practitioners.

Criterion 1: Maintains an unwavering priority of establishing and fostering an environment that tends to the Whole Child: healthy, safe, engaged, supported, and challenged

Although recent emphasis on student achievement has resulted in a renewed focus on effective practices of teaching and learning, it has also yielded an unintended consequence: a call for educators to address the Whole Child. Leading that charge, ASCD launched its Whole Child Initiative in 2007 to "change the conversation about education from a focus on narrowly defined academic achievement to one that promotes the long-term development and success of children" (ASCD, 2015). Administrators have a significant influential role in ensuring the school and community embrace the Whole Child tenets, working to create an environment in which each student is healthy, safe, engaged, supported, and challenged. By maintaining a global perspective, realizing that college and career readiness can be measured by more than a single test score, and leading policies and discussions that address each student as a comprehensive and unique human being, principals as engagers can truly act on behalf of every child within the school community.

ENGAGING LEADERSHIP IN ACTION

The staff of Magnolia Elementary School in Joppa, Maryland (a suburb of Baltimore), is convinced that its students—every single one of them—will be successful. With over 90 percent of students qualifying for free or reduced-price lunch, the school community has rallied together to support the Whole Child. Principal Patricia Mason credits the vision statement—"Reaching, Teaching, Learning . . . Changing Lives"—and the beliefs of the adults for what has been a remarkable success story.

The staff reaches its 500 students by splitting the campus into "houses," enabling teachers and support staff to create tight bonds with their students. A community garden, partnerships with local artists, the University of Maryland, and faith-based organizations all augment the effect of their Positive Behavioral Intervention and Support approaches and the integration of the tenets of Whole Child education.

A focus on Whole Brain teaching, an initiative led by teachers, ensures lessons that are engaging and rigorous. In fact, teacher leadership is a theme that comes up often in conversations about Magnolia. Principal Mason would have it no other way. Under her empowering guidance,

Magnolia was the recipient of the 2015 Vision in Action: The ASCD Whole Child Award, as well as a Maryland School of Character for 2015.

School district leaders and principal supervisors have a similar responsibility, as their scope of influence extends throughout the entire community and all of its principals. By creating the structures and systems that allow school principals to offer individualized learning options, provide professional learning opportunities for leaders and staff throughout the district, and set standards for implementing the Whole Child tenets, district leaders can build a system that tends to the Whole Child (Brown, 2008). Principals will need support as they delve into this work, making the district's role critical to the success of the venture.

Criterion 2: Creates and cultivates partnerships within the parent, district, business, political, and greater community spheres to support the achievement of the school's mission and vision

As we have mentioned before, the phrase "It takes a village to raise a child" is apropos to education. Even though business partners, community members, and political allies can provide much-needed resources to bolster a school's education programs, involving the greater community—including parents and family members—reaps another benefit: collectively held beliefs and goals for student success. Hattie suggests that "schools need to work in partnership with parents to make their expectations appropriately high and challenging, then work in partnership with children and the home to realize, and even surpass, these expectations" (2009, p. 70).

So how do principals effectively partner with parents and the external school community? Outreach to invite participation, maintain open communication, and create opportunities for involvement in governance help to build connections that strengthen support for the school and its mission (Marzano, 2003). Principals must seek partnerships with the village; rarely is it the other way around.

ENGAGING LEADERSHIP IN ACTION

You don't need to scroll too far down a newsfeed to find a commentary that is less than flattering to education. In the case of Prim Walters, assuming the principalship at Sun Valley Elementary, a designated turnaround school in Washoe County, Nevada, provided ample opportunity to restore the public's faith and belief in our schools. As an individual drawn to adults and building connections, coaching, and growing others, Walters used her position to champion this message: "Our school is the heart of the community and a place of safety."

By calling to introduce herself to local businesses, ordering staff lunches from the deli down the street, encouraging staff (including herself) to conduct home visits, and using social media to publicize school successes, she began a methodical process of building a network of mutual support. Walters uses optimism and enthusiasm to draw people together. "People want something to believe in. They want to be part of success. And they want to be inspired. As the principal, I hold tremendous power to influence this synergy." In the end, the school's success will add to its position as a neighborhood beacon of hope.

At a larger scale, the district office must likewise recruit, engage, and maintain meaningful relationships throughout the community. More directly, principal supervisors can support the efforts of building principals by making introductions, prioritizing these efforts, and providing examples of fruitful connections other schools have built. District leadership can further support the community-minded efforts of building leaders by emphasizing the importance of engager behaviors: messaging the vision, enlisting stakeholder involvement, inviting the public into the school, and proactively handling public relations duties. Savvy school leaders know that a highly informed and engaged community is essential to closing the achievement gap (Price, 2008)—this is at the heart of the principal's role as Engager.

Criterion 3: Drives and navigates positive change by assessing, analyzing, and anticipating emerging trends and implementing change-savvy techniques with staff and the school community

Noted business management guru W. Edwards Deming is credited as saying, "It is not necessary to change. Survival is not mandatory." Of course, Deming also quipped, "Change would be easy if it were not for people." In that spirit, school leaders understand one of the most fundamental elements of our business is, indeed, constant change. Anyone who has been in the field for any length of time has experienced innumerable changes, from class rosters to standards, from leadership structures to curriculum, and from personnel to the expected growth and development of the children in our care. In order to manage the change process productively, principals must negotiate short-term goals with long-term vision, prepare and encourage staff to embrace the reality of change, and address the school community's cultural readiness and hunger for positive, exciting opportunities for change—and progress (Reeves, 2009). Every school exists within its own particular context, so the nature and rate of change will vary from building to building. Principals lead the understanding and development of changes that lead to the accomplishment of the shared vision.

ENGAGING LEADERSHIP IN ACTION

When Taj Jensen, Washington's National Distinguished Principal honoree in 2015, was tapped to lead a turnaround at Tyee Park Elementary School in the Clover Park (Washington) School District, he knew the position came with an expectation of initiating significant change. Facing severe sanctions under state and federal accountability measures, Tyee Park was ripe for a turnaround. Jensen met with, listened to, and learned about every stakeholder and group in the school community. Gauging the context and need, he launched an aggressive change plan.

He set rigorous expectations for staff. He raised the bar for student achievement. He banned excuses. He called upon a moral imperative. He invited those not fully committed to the cause to move elsewhere. "Communication is key," stated Jensen. "Everything is clearly articulated to staff. There are no hidden punches. All staff are in the loop all the time."

With the table set, he rolled up his sleeves and led the brigade. Jensen redoubled the staff's focus on data analysis, goal setting, and professional capacity building. "As the landscape of this school shifts, I will adapt my approach to meet our changing needs. For now, I'm emphasizing the mission and having a lot of fierce conversations." If past performance is any indicator, future success awaits.

District leadership is similarly required to support principals as they engage in this challenging, and often unsettling, work. Because of the relentless nature of change, educators (teachers and principals alike) frequently feel as if they are aiming at a moving target. Principal supervisors and district leaders can help by clarifying goals and keeping the long-term vision consistent. That stability, at the very least, offers some comfort to those whose ground is moving beneath their feet. Supporting principals by viewing change as a force consisting of "great rapidity and nonlinearity on the one hand and equally great potential for creative breakthroughs on the other"

(Fullan, 2001, p. 31), district officials can help develop a leadership lens for current and future leaders.

Criterion 4: Safeguards community values, ethics, and equitable practices, advocating for all children and displaying an appreciation for diversity

As the figurehead of the school, it is the principal's responsibility to speak and act as the chief advocate for all children. In policies, procedures, and practice, school leaders must eschew the notion that "demography is destiny" (Payzant, 2011) and pull out all stops to ensure the success of every student in the school. Socioeconomic status, race, language barriers, and a host of other factors have long impeded progress for many of our system's students; however, in the eyes, heart, and influence of passionate, committed, supportive leaders, they are secondary descriptors of children with bright futures and brighter dreams.

Coauthor Deborah Childs-Bowen extolls the virtue of equitable practice, stating, "For generations, the 3 Rs—reading, 'riting, and 'rithmetic—have driven education . . . now it's time to add 4 new Rs to the education lexicon: respect, responsibility, relationships, and results" (2006, p. 2). Principals can engage and influence their teaching staffs, the community, and even the students themselves to embrace an educational experience that is socially just and equitable, celebrates the wonderful diversity within the student body, and champions a belief that all students will emerge as winners in the game of life.

ENGAGING LEADERSHIP IN ACTION

When Marc Cohen was named ASCD's Outstanding Young Educator Award honoree in 2009, it was a tribute to his passionate work toward eliminating the racial predictability of student achievement at Dr. Martin Luther King, Jr. Middle School in the Montgomery County (Maryland) Public Schools. Just a few years later, Cohen carried that passion and a similar goal to his principalship at Seneca Valley High School. Leading for equity, talking about race, and discussing deeply held values can be scary work, yet it is critical for meaningful school improvement.

Cohen makes explicit his concerns and vision for establishing an environment that is equitable and overflows with high expectations for all students. It is common for staff and visitors to hear him state, quite passionately, "I believe that each and every student that walks through the doors of our school has the ability to achieve at high academic levels, and it is my responsibility as their principal to make sure that they're provided with world-class instruction to help them live up to their fullest potential." Staff have adopted this belief, and the results show improvements in almost all corners of the school. Living the commitment sets the tone, according to Cohen: "Never underestimate the power of relentlessness."

School district officials must support their principals by establishing policies and procedures that support the notion that all children can be—and will be, under our watch—successful. They can do this by providing school leaders with the research, leeway, and tools to help them close the attitude gap, which exceptional school leader Baruti Kafele defines as "the gap between those students who have the will to strive for academic excellence and those who do not" (2013, p. 13). Interestingly, there is an attitude gap for teachers, principals, and other adults in the school systems as well, and it is here that savvy school leaders can effect some monumental changes.

Criterion 5: Develops policies and practices that cultivate staff as reflective practitioners

As we think, so will we go. We need only to examine the antonyms of key phrases to highlight the importance of the art of self-reflection: the opposite of building awareness is practicing ignorance; the opposite of planning intentionally is doing things absentmindedly; the opposite of assessing progress is proceeding heedlessly; and the opposite of being responsive is continuing regardless.

Are those the terms we'd like to use when describing our professional educators? Rather than constantly reacting to the situations that befall them, reflective practitioners can, in the words of John Dewey, "act on the basis of the absent and the future" (1910, p. 14). They can predict, infer, reason, analyze, and imagine. Principals understand the value of such thoughtfulness, and they intentionally craft ways to develop the intentionality and self-reflective abilities of their staffs. By doing so, and by developing a growth mindset, leaders can reinforce the notion that "effort is the key to success" (Dweck, 2006).

ENGAGING LEADERSHIP IN ACTION

Building teachers' reflective capacity has long been a passion for coauthor Alisa Simeral, a turnaround coach working with Sun Valley Elementary School in Reno, Nevada. Partnering with the school support team (principal, counselor, ELL specialist, special education teacher, psychologist, and instructional coaches), Simeral introduced a quarterly student-focused reflection meeting process. Four times a year, each teacher sits down with the team and explains every student—as a learner and as a young person—from every angle imaginable.

Scrutinizing attendance, behavior, coursework data, anecdotal records, teacher observations, and the success rates of various strategies, teachers engage in rich, collaborative reflection with the team. What was initially uncomfortable for staff (expecting to "report" on student performance only) has become a transformative exercise in engaging in the Reflective Cycle: teachers build awareness of their students' needs, select teaching strategies deliberately, note what's working and what's not working, and refine their practice to meet the learning goals of individual students. And it's caught on. According to Simeral, "Teachers are huddling together in the hallways and staff room to brainstorm and problem solve. Talking about student learning and reflecting on practice is the new norm."

A school district is simply a school on a much larger scale (depending on the size of the district, of course). Though it might seem simpler to train "yes men" and create a culture of followers, long-term success of a school district is dependent on the ability of its human capital— its people—to think critically and engage in the Reflective Cycle (Hall & Simeral, 2015). At the risk of defining a practice by using the practice as an example, the application of this book and the many strategies herein is a clear illustration of that undertaking. District officials create the environment in which principals can learn, practice, and apply procedures that value and encourage divergent thought, open discussions, transparency, involvement, and innovation.

Growing as an Engager: Strategies for Reflective Growth

In the following sections, we offer several strategies for building principals' leadership capacity within this role. Each provides the opportunity for the principal (Pathway One) and the district-level supervisors (Pathway Two) to clarify the work and streamline all efforts toward the long-term outcome: develop and refine reflective practices while simultaneously augmenting expertise in these criteria. Simply put, we're aiming for principals to operate in the Refinement stage as engagers.

The strategies we offer in Figure 5.1 are but a sampling of the many avenues to approach growth within each criterion. The strategies we have selected deliver high-leverage, universal results, and many of them include tools, templates, proto-cols, and forms that you can find in Appendix B and online at www.ascd.org/ASCD/pdf/books/TPI2016.pdf. It is our intent to provide you with immediately actionable, easily implemented strategies that bridge the gap between research and application. Strategies with a support resource in Appendix B are marked with an asterisk (*).

FIGURE 5.1

Principal as Engager Strategy Schematic

	CRITERION 1: Maintains an unwavering priority of establishing and fostering an environment that tends to the Whole Child: healthy, safe, engaged, supported, and challenged.	CRITERION 2: Creates and cultivates partnerships within the parent, district, business, political, and greater community spheres to support the achievement of the school's mission and vision.	CRITERION 3: Drives and navigates positive change by assessing, analyzing, and anticipating emerging trends and implementing change-savvy techniques with staff and the school community.	CRITERION 4: Safeguards community values, ethics, and equitable practices, advocating for all children and displaying an appreciation for diversity.	CRITERION 5: Develops policies and practices that cultivate staff as reflective practitioners.
PATHWAY ONE: SCHOOL LEVEL	• Integrate a Focus on the Whole Child into SIPs • Take an Inventory of Potential Whole Child Partners*	• Analyze the Audiences* • Tap into Existing Resources	• Determine Change Readiness* • Confront Fears, Embrace Hopes*	• Reflect on Equity Leadership Skills* • Support Teachers in Connecting with Students*	• Engage in Reflective Self-Talk • Build Reflection Through Lesson Study*
PATHWAY TWO: DISTRICT LEVEL	• Prioritize Whole Child Approaches* • Learn and Work Together	• Collaborate Beyond School Boundaries • Guide School-Level Communication Plans*	• Lead Change Management Efforts* • Establish Partnerships to Manage Change*	• Adopt a Framework for High-Poverty Schools • Ensure School-wide Ethical Behavior* • Conduct an Equity Audit*	• Role-Play from a Different Perspective • Adopt a Model to Build Reflective Capacity*

Note: Strategies with an asterisk (*) include a tool/template/protocol/form in Appendix B.

With a thorough understanding of the role and the criteria that contribute to effective instructional leadership within the role of an engager a good place to begin is with an honest self-assessment. Reflect on each criterion as a separate piece of your leadership puzzle. Within each criterion, we have added a brief self-assessment guide to facilitate leaders' exploration of their current thinking and technical proficiency. In the Reflective Leadership Planning Template (found in Appendix A and downloadable at www.ascd.org/ASCD/pdf/books/TPI2016.pdf), we suggest that principals (or assistant principals or aspiring principals) sit down with their supervisors/mentors/coaches and collaboratively record a narrative of their own current reality, including where they operate on the Principal's Continuum of Self-Reflection.

After scrutinizing the sample strategies that follow and collaboratively brainstorming additional strategies (with colleagues, supervisors, and others in your professional learning network), use the Reflective Leadership Planning Template to document the powerful steps you will take to develop your (or your principal's) growth as a reflective engager. There is great strength in the dialogue, collaboration, and partnership in this goal-setting endeavor; utilize the resources at your disposal to create and refine a clear, focused, reflection-oriented plan.

Criterion 1

Guiding Question: How can we foster an environment that tends to the Whole Child?

Theory of Action: Each child's path to success is as unique and complex as the child himself or herself. Effective schools believe that every student must be healthy, safe, engaged, supported, and challenged. If the principal maintains a priority of fostering an environment that tends to the Whole Child tenets, then every student will be adequately prepared for current success and future ambitions (Parrett & Budge, 2012).

In Figure 5.2, the Principal's Continuum of Self-Reflection describes the depth of thinking related to leadership actions in this criterion. To the right of each stage is the focus behavior for developing reflective capacity within the criterion. Refer to the Reflective Cycle (Figure 2.3, p. 17) and the focused reflective questions (Figure 2.4, p. 22) for more guidance.

Pathway One: School Level

Integrate a Focus on the Whole Child into SIPs

ASCD's Whole Child approach is a framework for sustainable school improvement. The Whole Child School Improvement Tool is a needs assessment built on the tenets of healthy, safe, engaged, supported, and challenged (for more information,

FIGURE 5.2

P-CSR: *Engager Criterion 1*

UNAWARE STAGE	BUILD AWARENESS	CONSCIOUS STAGE	PLAN INTENTIONALLY	ACTION STAGE	ACCURATELY ASSESS IMPACT	REFINEMENT STAGE	BECOME RESPONSIVE
Manages the day-to-day operations of the school without emphasis on Whole Child tenets.		Demonstrates awareness of Whole Child tenets without specific plans to address them.		Enacts structures and procedures to address the Whole Child tenets.		Maintains a priority of fostering an environment that tends to the Whole Child tenets.	

visit ASCD's Whole Child website at http://www.wholechildeducation.org/). The tenets and aligned components can support principals as they work with their staff and community to integrate the framework into the school improvement planning process. Principals can start by completing the needs assessment found at the aforementioned website themselves and then having other administrators on their team do the same. The team can examine the results to determine where there is agreement about the most pressing or important areas of need. The next step would be to have the staff complete the needs assessment. Use several faculty meetings to debrief the results. Have staff review the results in small groups using a data review protocol. Leave the faculty meeting with agreed-upon next steps for how the data will be used to inform (or be included in) the SIP.

Take an Inventory of Potential Whole Child Partners*

Embracing a Whole Child approach is best accomplished as a collaborative venture with multiple partners from beyond the school walls. Principals and the leadership team can work together to create a list of school-community partnerships that might support the Whole Child tenets within the SIP. Brainstorm and discuss how each potential partner could provide support. Use the following categories for the list: community college/universities, business/corporate, service learning, health and human services, multi-age services, cultural organizations, and religious organizations (a Whole Child Partners Inventory is included in Appendix B.23 for your use). Following the brainstorming and discussion, assign team members—some of whom may already have connections and relationships with individuals and organizations on the list—to reach out to the potential partners and invite them to an initial meeting to learn more about the Whole Child tenets and how they could benefit students and families.

Pathway Two: District Level

Prioritize Whole Child Approaches*

Integrating Whole Child problem solving and decision making into the work district leaders do with principals will ensure that the Whole Child tenets are viewed as an important aspect of the district's culture. Supervisors, coaches, and mentors can use the Whole Child Problem-Solving and Decision-Making Questions (Appendix B.24) in strategic planning sessions and leadership development meetings and retreats to support an improved focus on Whole Child systemic outcomes. Principals can then take their learning and carry it back to their buildings, posing the same questions to staff to further highlight the value and importance of this approach.

Learn and Work Together

In order to gain an understanding of the Whole Child resources that are available to school leaders, coaches and district officials can access the free Whole Child School Improvement Tool (available at http://www.wholechildeducation.org/). After learning about the available resources, coaches and district leaders can create coaching strategies and action steps that will support principals in integrating the Whole Child approach into the school's mission and vision, its work with the community, and the SIP.

Criterion 2

Guiding Question: How can we engage the entire community to support our collective vision?

Theory of Action: Education is a community's shared responsibility. Research and common sense substantiate the importance of active community involvement in children's education (Price, 2008). If the principal creates, cultivates, and sustains partnerships with outside agencies and constituents to support the school's mission and vision, then the entire community will unite in its efforts to maximize student success.

In Figure 5.3, the Principal's Continuum of Self-Reflection describes the depth of thinking related to leadership actions in this criterion. To the right of each stage is the focus behavior for developing reflective capacity within the criterion. Refer to the Reflective Cycle (Figure 2.3, p.17) and the focused reflective questions (Figure 2.4, p. 22) for more guidance.

FIGURE 5.3

P-CSR: Engager Criterion 2

UNAWARE STAGE		CONSCIOUS STAGE		ACTION STAGE		REFINEMENT STAGE	
Does not seek out opportunities to partner with outside agencies and constituents.	BUILD AWARENESS	Partners with outside constituents on an as-needed or as-requested basis.	PLAN INTENTIONALLY	Builds relationships with outside agencies and constituents intentionally.	ACCURATELY ASSESS IMPACT	Creates, cultivates, and sustains partnerships with outside agencies and constituents to support the school's mission and vision.	BECOME RESPONSIVE

Pathway One: School Level

Analyze the Audiences*

Ongoing, open communication is a two-way street. Effective principals provide tools and guidelines for both key parties to discuss their communication needs: for staff to identify their perceptions of the strengths and challenges of outreach to the community, and for different community groups to share their desires and fears about connecting with the school. By collecting that feedback (by visiting or hosting various constituent group meetings) and then acting on it, principals demonstrate their integrity and the value they place on maintaining effective communication channels. With community feedback in hand, principals can lead faculty meetings at the beginning of the year, collecting staff impressions of school community demographics, politics, and cultures; analyzing how the school reaches out to constituents; and brainstorming creative ways of connecting with various groups. As a result of this activity, develop and distribute guidelines for connecting with the community during the year. The guidelines will bolster the commitment to community and school collaboration. The Customized Strategic Communication Plan (Appendix B.2) is included for your use.

Tap into Existing Resources

Cultivating an active, involved collection of partners-in-education can provide immeasurable support to a school's pursuit of its mission, vision, and SIP goals. Effective principals can engage this network by capitalizing on existing resources within the school community. Often, schools are situated in communities with multiple businesses, office buildings, organizations, and agencies. The mission of a neighbor-hood school is such that these potential partners would be willing allies if the oppor-tunity (or the invitation) presented itself. Principals can make the first contact by inviting representatives to school events, frequenting their establishments, and sim-ply stopping by to introduce themselves. After these interactions, principals can use social media platforms such as Facebook and Instagram to share images, show back-ing, and offer gratitude for the support. As the relationships strengthen, principals can request a formal partnership commitment. By investigating the strengths and resources available in these partnerships, the school can address valuable needs that might otherwise go untended.

Pathway Two: District Level

Collaborate Beyond School Boundaries

Porterfield and Carnes state, "In many of our communities, 80 percent of the cit-izens do not have children in the public schools. In order to maintain the support of the community, we must be sure that these citizens have accurate information about the schools and feel a connection to the schools and their success" (2008, p. 154). District staff can organize principals in adjacent neighborhoods to strategize and work collaboratively to educate and communicate with the larger community about their schools' mission and related activities. Principals can collaboratively write and publish articles in local homeowners' venues (e.g., blogs, newsletters). Principals in feeder patterns can collaboratively present to articulate the K–12 approach and verti-cal connections for students and families at association, condominium, and commu-nity center meetings. Feeder-pattern principals can also hold a back-to-school-night session in the community as a way to provide outreach to families unable to come to the school facility. In this way, principals are sharing responsibility for their commu-nity and maximizing their time.

Guide School-Level Communication Plans*

High-quality district-level leadership development support always includes sup-port for principals in creating a customized strategic communication plan for their school. Principal supervisors can provide guidance, coaching, and feedback for prin-cipals as they develop their plan. The plan could include communication strategies and vehicles, along with target audiences, in seven areas: (1) providing informa-tion about school programs, events, and activities; (2) providing information about student learning, student progress, and achievement; (3) providing information about helping children learn and succeed in school; (4) fostering a sense of belonging for all students; (5) maintaining proactive efforts to secure positive media coverage and attention; (6) fostering a productive workplace and enhancing employees' professionalism and sense of community; and (7) creating meaningful opportunities for parent/family and school collaboration. The communication plan should be visible and used by all staff and other school stakeholders. A modified version of a template, focusing on instructional leadership goals, is included in Appendix B.25.

Criterion 3

Guiding Question: How can we lead the change process to have a positive effect on our work?

Theory of Action: Change is inevitable, and change, as noted by Hall and Simeral, "is a prerequisite for improvement" (2008, p. 6). Leaders are challenged with reframing the school culture to be eager participants in the change process. If the principal leads positive change by assessing, analyzing, and anticipating emerging trends, then the school will evolve and grow toward the common vision.

In Figure 5.4, the Principal's Continuum of Self-Reflection describes the depth of thinking related to leadership actions in this criterion. To the right of each stage is the focus behavior for developing reflective capacity within the criterion. Refer to the Reflective Cycle (Figure 2.3, p. 17) and the focused reflective questions (Figure 2.4, p. 22) for more guidance.

FIGURE 5.4

P-CSR: Engager Criterion 3

UNAWARE STAGE	BUILD AWARENESS	CONSCIOUS STAGE	PLAN INTENTIONALLY	ACTION STAGE	ACCURATELY ASSESS IMPACT	REFINEMENT STAGE	BECOME RESPONSIVE
Allows change to halt actions and/or interrupt school operations.		Resists change and/or reacts to changing contexts with immediate actions.		Embraces change as an opportunity to learn and grow.		Leads positive change processes by assessing, analyzing, and anticipating emerging trends.	

Pathway One: School Level

Determine Change Readiness*

Change is inevitable, and in education it can be said that change is the nature of the business. Before initiating a major change, however, effective principals determine their school's readiness for the new practice, process, or program. The information yielded from a survey such as the Change Readiness Rubric (Appendix B.26) will inform the principal and leadership team of the school staff's openness, eagerness, and stability to embrace a potentially significant change. Use or modify this tool to gather key data, including information about the school's history, the perceived need for change, the staff's willingness to change, the faith in leadership, the change plan, and the skills necessary to implement the change. That information, in turn, can be used to create a plan to create and sustain the conditions suitable for major change implementation.

Confront Fears, Embrace Hopes*

Even the most collaborative principals know that there will be times when they must simply enact certain changes; they are unavoidable realities of the profession. During those times, school leaders can positively position staff to understand the new expectations, the rationale behind them, and the impact the change will have upon individuals and systems. To bolster staff's readiness, allow staff members to express their "worst fears" and "best hopes" for the change. This is most efficiently and safely accomplished in small groups (grade-level teams or departments).

After sharing the facts and details about the change, invite staff to write down and share their "worst fears." By doing this, and by providing time for staff to also write down and share their "best hopes," principals model an openness to all perspectives and validate the emotional reactions to change, both pro and con. A simple tool, Fears and Hopes: A Change Readiness Perspective (Appendix B.27), is available to guide these conversations. Use the information shared to determine what supports are needed to allay staff's fears and to celebrate the realizations of their hopes as they implement the new change.

Pathway Two: District Level

Lead Change Management Efforts*

Because change is such a prevalent force in education, savvy district leaders are sure to include wide theoretical frameworks for change management in their ongoing professional learning opportunities for principals. Identifying similarities and differences between John Kotter's six stages (Kotter, 1996) or William Bridges's three stages of change (Bridges, 1991) and investigating Michael Fullan's six secrets of change (Fullan, 2008) will help principals recognize culture shifts that accompany (or precede) significant changes.

Have principals provide several anecdotes to note in which stage their staff is most likely functioning. Using the Change Theory Highlights tool (Appendix B.28), principal coaches can then assist principals in developing actions to lead and manage staff through the change. Coaches can help principals plan how to leverage professional development and collaborative learning communities to advance the transformation.

Establish Partnerships to Manage Change*

District leaders have a responsibility to support teams of principals as they engage with the struggles associated with managing change. Principal supervisors can embed change management leadership development during principals' meetings or regularly scheduled leadership development sessions. By assigning principals to Communities of Practice by feeder pattern or grade levels, district leaders can provide ongoing support in a collaborative environment. Set aside some time at each gathering to have principal teams list and discuss the major changes they are leading, planning for, or anticipating in their schools. The Communities of Practice come to consensus on whether the change is first-order (simple to implement and requires technical work) or second-order change (more complex and requires mindset adaptations). If a change is determined to be second-order, then the team uses the Change Management Questionnaire (Appendix B.29) to plan how they will celebrate successes, address challenges, and remove obstacles. Prioritize the time necessary for the Communities of Practice to have regular check-ins during the year to support one another in implementing changes.

Criterion 4

Guiding Question: How can we celebrate each child's uniqueness, ensure equity, and model our collective values?

Theory of Action: Every child is unique and special—as learners and as human beings (Tomlinson, 2014). We must treat them that way, expect them to be successful, and engage the adults in the system to act in accordance with that expectation. If the principal safeguards community values and displays an appreciation for diversity and social justice by advocating for all students through equitable education practices, then every student will have the opportunity to achieve personal excellence.

In Figure 5.5, the Principal's Continuum of Self-Reflection describes the depth of thinking related to leadership actions in this criterion. To the right of each stage is the focus behavior for developing reflective capacity within the criterion. Refer to the Reflective Cycle (Figure 2.3, p. 17) and the focused reflective questions (Figure 2.4, p. 22) for more guidance.

FIGURE 5.5

P-CSR: *Engager Criterion 4*

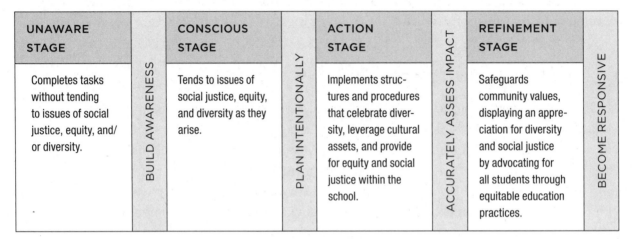

UNAWARE STAGE	BUILD AWARENESS	CONSCIOUS STAGE	PLAN INTENTIONALLY	ACTION STAGE	ACCURATELY ASSESS IMPACT	REFINEMENT STAGE	BECOME RESPONSIVE
Completes tasks without tending to issues of social justice, equity, and/ or diversity.		Tends to issues of social justice, equity, and diversity as they arise.		Implements structures and procedures that celebrate diversity, leverage cultural assets, and provide for equity and social justice within the school.		Safeguards community values, displaying an appreciation for diversity and social justice by advocating for all students through equitable education practices.	

Pathway One: School Level

Reflect on Equity Leadership Skills*

Achievement gaps in education are famous for their prevalence. Effective principals, serving in the role of Engager, hold staunchly to their conviction that such gaps should not just be reduced–they should be eradicated. The driving force of such leaders is to ensure equitable access to an exceptional educational experience for every child, every moment. In the *Courageous Equity Leadership Toolkit,* Edwin Javius writes, "Getting to equity means applying additional or different resources to ensure all students receive what they need to reach grade level standards" (2009, p. 16).

In order to ensure equity, principals and other building leaders must first probe and reflect on their own equity leadership professional growth needs. Using the Equity Leadership Reflection Rubric (Appendix B.30), principals and school leaders can examine their mindset, knowledge, skills, and actions through an equity lens. They must then review the results and integrate the needs in this area into an individual leadership development plan that includes steps they will take to build their competency and enrich their equity leadership practices.

Support Teachers in Connecting with Students*

The powerful quote "No significant learning occurs without a significant relationship" (Comer, 1995) serves as a rallying cry for anyone interested in ethical, equitable educational practices. Principals must make sure that teachers connect with students to ensure equity; access to high levels of learning; and an appreciation for diversity in thinking, behaviors, beliefs, and cultures. To support this end, principals can facilitate a professional learning experience in small-group meetings or at a faculty meeting to make sure all instructional staff understand how to incorporate the uniqueness of their students into their instructional planning. We have included two tools that address this process. The Who Am I? Student Self-Assessment (Appendix B.31) allows students to identify and express their special qualities, background information, academic skills, and interests. The My Student Matrix (Appendix B.32) compiles information about students in a class to help the teacher and students understand what they have in common and what is unique about each person. By celebrating both, educators can build a stronger community, design learning experiences that meet students' needs, and structure lessons in ways that contribute to all students' success.

Pathway Two: District Level

Adopt a Framework for High-Poverty Schools

Making sure there is a research base for what leaders in high-poverty schools do to ensure student success is an essential responsibility of principal supervisors, mentors, and coaches. They can begin by organizing an action-oriented book study among building principals. One option that we highly recommend is the book and study guide for *Turning High Poverty Schools into High Performing Schools* (Parrett & Budge, 2012). Supervisors, mentors, and coaches should also develop face-to-face or virtual implementation check-ins as part of the action-oriented book study. The check-ins should focus on ensuring that participants are applying practices and policies in their schools from what they are learning. Include the use of job-embedded coaching and feedback support along the way, and make sure to integrate collegial sharing, celebrating, and problem solving in action-oriented book study discussions.

Ensure Schoolwide Ethical Behavior*

Making sure that principals have ethical practices and policies in place at their schools is essential to ensure the success of the principal, along with the teachers and students they lead. Principal supervisors, coaches, and mentors can integrate the use of the Ethical Leadership Action Steps Guide (Appendix B.33) as they provide job-embedded coaching to their principals. During scheduled site visits, meetings, or leadership gatherings, designate part of the conversation to the status of equitable, student-focused practices that ensure social justice. The use of the checklist will help surface concerns that might otherwise go unaddressed, ensuring that ethical practices are discussed naturally as part of the coaching experience.

Conduct an Equity Audit*

District leaders can promote and safeguard equitable practices by engaging in equity audits with principals. These types of audits help reveal inequities within a particular school or throughout the district. Questions from an Equity Audit tool (Appendix B.34) return data that indicate whether certain populations of students or staff are over- and underrepresented in key areas, such as special education, AP or honors courses, remedial classes, and clubs and activities. Attendance, behavior, and coursework data also indicate whether there might be a need for additional attention paid to ensuring equitable practices. Teacher assignments, such as years of experience, demographics, certifications, and other characteristics are linked to student enrollment and achievement to reveal connections that might not otherwise be noted. The data collected from an equity audit becomes a leadership tool for district-level administrators to engage principals and school leaders in inquiry about the issues of equity and social justice.

Criterion 5

Guiding Question: How can we build our individual and collective capacity as reflective practitioners?

Theory of Action: The more reflective we are, the more effective we are. One of the principal's most vital charges is to build the reflective capacity of the staff "by helping them reflect on their practices and make positive changes in their classrooms that will improve student learning" (Hall & Simeral, 2008, p. 31). If the principal leads the implementation of policies and practices that cultivate staff as reflective practitioners, then staff will be better equipped to ensure high levels of student learning.

In Figure 5.6, the Principal's Continuum of Self-Reflection describes the depth of thinking related to leadership actions in this criterion. To the right of each stage is the focus behavior for developing reflective capacity within the criterion. Refer to the Reflective Cycle (Figure 2.3, p. 17) and the focused reflective questions (Figure 2.4, p. 22) for more guidance.

Pathway One: School Level

Engage in Reflective Self-Talk

Reflective practice, or "thinking about your own practice and enabling others to think about theirs," offers an opportunity for principals to make decisions with confidence (Lambert, 2003, p. 7). Pausing, reflecting, and considering alternatives lead

FIGURE 5.6

P-CSR: Engager Criterion 5

UNAWARE STAGE	BUILD AWARENESS	CONSCIOUS STAGE	PLAN INTENTIONALLY	ACTION STAGE	ACCURATELY ASSESS PROGRESS	REFINEMENT STAGE	BE RESPONSIVE
Does not see a need to cultivate staff as reflective practitioners.		Is aware of the need for policies and practices that will cultivate staff as reflective practitioners.		Collaboratively develops policies and practices that cultivate staff as reflective practitioners.		Leads the implementation of policies and practices that cultivate staff as reflective practitioners.	

to greater clarity, so a principal skilled at self-talk is more apt to align decisions with the vision. Principals can build this skill by reflecting on the very questions that will likely be posed by stakeholders when considering decisions: How does this proposed action support the vision we have adopted? How is it aligned? What's in it for me? What impact will it have on our journey? What options have I considered? How have I communicated my intentions? What might go wrong? How might our constituents feel about the proposal? By considering these questions and more, principals can equip themselves with a broader understanding of the situation, thereby situating themselves for a more positive outcome.

Build Reflection Through Lesson Study*

Principals who integrate the use of lesson study into expectations for teacher collaboration and reflection will most likely see positive results in the classroom. There are many models of lesson study that allow teams of teachers, coaches, and administrators to analyze all aspects of a given lesson, paying particular attention to the intended learning outcomes, actual learning outcomes, and actions that caused learning to happen (or not happen). Effective principals guide their instructional staff through a Lesson Study Protocol (such as the one in Appendix B.35) to quickly and directly identify the key cause-and-effect relationship within a lesson. As teams collect and view video of agreed-upon classroom lessons, they consider questions that identify instructional practices, student look-fors, evidence of learning, and other structural pieces. The Lesson Study Protocol also provides guiding questions that encourage reflection and lead participants to plan their next steps.

Pathway Two: District Level

Role-Play from a Different Perspective

"We don't see things as they are, we see them as we are." This quote, from acclaimed author Anaïs Nin, reminds us of the importance of our own viewpoint (1961, p. 124). To help school leaders broaden their perspective and see others' points of view, principal supervisors can engage their principals in a deconstruction of a thorny situation (e.g., the potential elimination of field trips throughout the school district). The situation can be current (with names redacted), based on an event from the past, or completely fictional. During a principals' meeting, have school leaders examine the situation from four to six different points of view. Have them take on any of the following roles: student, parent, senior citizen, teacher, superintendent, news reporter, business owner, school board member, district alumnus, or random bystander. First, have them note some of the possible feelings, comments, and concerns of their role. Then pose the situation and have them respond according to the designated role. Staying in character, the school leader might respond, "As a senior citizen, I'm concerned that . . . ." At the conclusion, have principals note any revelations they had while considering those new perspectives.

Adopt a Model to Build Reflective Capacity*

Self-reflection is a valuable skill. Not only does one's ability to reflect deeply, accurately, and frequently lead to greater results, but as a skill, reflection can be developed and strengthened. Every member of the school district, including superintendents, principals, teachers, classified staff, and anyone else with an approved ID badge, can become more reflective—and more effective in their professional responsibilities. Investigating our preferred model, outlined in *Building Teachers' Capacity for Success* (Hall & Simeral, 2008) and *Teach, Reflect, Learn* (Hall & Simeral, 2015), will uncover the language and tools essential to engaging in deep, accurate, and frequent reflection across the district. District-level officials can guide principals to develop strategies for embedding reflection in every aspect of district operations. Educators throughout the system can embrace the language and habits of reflective behaviors, and using the Reflective Cycle Goals Chart (Appendix B.36) helps link the components of the Reflective Cycle to each stage along the Continuum of Self-Reflection.

Where to Start

Gaining a comprehensive understanding of the principal's role as Engager is one thing; synthesizing the complex bank of strategies into the nuanced context of a particular school or district is another thing altogether. Before we offer a suggested course of action, let us be clear: it is neither our intent nor our expectation that school or district leaders take the strategies discussed in this chapter as "marching orders," proceeding through the list and checking them off when "complete." Rather, they are options for growing as an engager while simultaneously developing as a reflective practitioner.

In the following section (see Figure 5.7), we have included a self-assessment guide to help provide clarity and direction for your next steps. Though this can be used as a self-directed growth tool, it is preferable to utilize it collaboratively—with peers, colleagues, and supervisors—in order to extract the maximum benefit. For principal supervisors and district officials, this guide can be particularly useful when sitting down with building leaders to set goals, analyze performance, and create a plan to build leadership capacity within the role of Engager

Directions for the Self-Assessment Guide

1. Review the stages of the Principal's Continuum of Self-Reflection (P-CSR) along each criterion.
2. Highlight words or phrases and jot down notes regarding your reflective tendencies and professional practice within each criterion.
3. Depending on the stage of the P-CSR at which you believe you are operating, identify the action from the Reflective Cycle that requires your focus.
   a. If you are operating in the Unaware stage, your goal is to build awareness.
   b. If you are operating in the Conscious stage, your goal is to plan intentionally.
   c. If you are operating in the Action stage, your goal is to assess impact.
   d. If you are operating in the Refinement stage, your goal is to become responsive.
4. Select a strategy from either Pathway One (school level) or Pathway Two (district level) that will help you address this criterion.
5. After completing this task for all four criteria within the principal's role as Engager, collaboratively select the one key criterion on which you are ready to focus.
6. Use the Reflective Leadership Planning Template (Appendix A) to create a thorough, robust plan for growing as an engager while simultaneously developing as a reflective practitioner.

FIGURE 5.7

Principal as Engager Self-Assessment Guide

	UNAWARE STAGE	CONSCIOUS STAGE	ACTION STAGE	REFINEMENT STAGE
CRITERION 1: Maintains an unwavering priority of establishing and fostering an environment that tends to the Whole Child: healthy, safe, engaged, supported, and challenged.	Manages the day-to-day operations of the school without emphasis on Whole Child tenets.	Demonstrates awareness of Whole Child tenets without specific plans to address them.	Enacts structures and procedures to address the Whole Child tenets.	Maintains a priority of fostering an environment that tends to the Whole Child tenets.

1. Why do you feel this stage is an accurate representation of your thinking about this criterion?

2. Which action from the Reflective Cycle requires your focus in order to grow as a reflective practitioner? (See Figure 2.3 for guidance.)

   Build Awareness   Plan Intentionally   Accurately Assess Progress   Be Responsive

3. Which strategy listed under Criterion 1 might best support your growth as you take action?

	UNAWARE STAGE	CONSCIOUS STAGE	ACTION STAGE	REFINEMENT STAGE
CRITERION 2: Creates and cultivates partnerships within the parent, district, business, political, and greater community spheres to support the achievement of the school's mission and vision.	Does not seek out opportunities to partner with outside agencies and constituents.	Partners with outside constituents on an as-needed or as-requested basis.	Builds relationships with outside agencies and constituents intentionally.	Creates, cultivates, and sustains partnerships with outside agencies and constituents to support the school's mission and vision.

1. Why do you feel this stage is an accurate representation of your thinking about this criterion?

2. Which action from the Reflective Cycle requires your focus in order to grow as a reflective practitioner? (See Figure 2.3 for guidance.)

   Build Awareness   Plan Intentionally   Accurately Assess Progress   Be Responsive

3. Which strategy listed under Criterion 2 might best support your growth as you take action?

	UNAWARE STAGE	CONSCIOUS STAGE	ACTION STAGE	REFINEMENT STAGE
CRITERION 3: Drives and navigates positive change by assessing, analyzing, and anticipating emerging trends and implementing change-savvy techniques with staff and the school community.	Allows change to halt actions and/or interrupt school operations.	Resists change and/or reacts to changing contexts with immediate actions.	Embraces change as an opportunity to learn and grow.	Leads positive change processes by assessing, analyzing, and anticipating emerging trends.

1. Why do you feel this stage is an accurate representation of your thinking about this criterion?

2. Which action from the Reflective Cycle requires your focus in order to grow as a reflective practitioner? (See Figure 2.3 for guidance.)

   Build Awareness   Plan Intentionally   Accurately Assess Progress   Be Responsive

3. Which strategy listed under Criterion 3 might best support your growth as you take action?

	UNAWARE STAGE	CONSCIOUS STAGE	ACTION STAGE	REFINEMENT STAGE
CRITERION 4: Safeguards community values, ethics, and equitable practices, advocating for all children and displaying an appreciation for diversity.	Completes tasks without tending to issues of social justice, equity, and/or diversity.	Tends to issues of social justice, equity, and diversity as they arise.	Implements structures and procedures that celebrate diversity, leverage cultural assets, and provide for equity and social justice within the school.	Safeguards community values, displaying an appreciation for diversity and social justice by advocating for all students through equitable education practices.

1. Why do you feel this stage is an accurate representation of your thinking about this criterion?
2. Which action from the Reflective Cycle requires your focus in order to grow as a reflective practitioner? (See Figure 2.3 for guidance.)
   Build Awareness   Plan Intentionally   Accurately Assess Progress   Be Responsive
3. Which strategy listed under Criterion 4 might best support your growth as you take action?

	UNAWARE STAGE	CONSCIOUS STAGE	ACTION STAGE	REFINEMENT STAGE
CRITERION 5: Develops policies and practices that cultivate staff as reflective practitioners.	Does not see a need to cultivate staff as reflective practitioners.	Is aware of the need for policies and practices that will cultivate staff as reflective practitioners.	Collaboratively develops policies and practices that cultivate staff as reflective practitioners.	Leads the implementation of policies and practices that cultivate staff as reflective practitioners.

1. Why do you feel this stage is an accurate representation of your thinking about this criterion?
2. Which action from the Reflective Cycle requires your focus in order to grow as a reflective practitioner? (See Figure 2.3 for guidance.)
   Build Awareness   Plan Intentionally   Accurately Assess Progress   Be Responsive
3. Which strategy listed under Criterion 5 might best support your growth as you take action?

CHAPTER 6
Principal as Learner and Collaborator

In addition to being the CLO—the Chief Learning Officer—the principal must also be the LL: the Lead Learner. The quest for continuous improvement starts at the top, and the principal must set an expectation for excellence and demonstrate an openness to learning, growing, innovating, sharing, and connecting. By modeling a growth mindset (Dweck, 2006), the principal as Learner and Collaborator ensures robust and continuous learning for everyone in the system: students, staff, administrators, and everyone in between. As Rick DuFour states, "Schools need leadership from principals who focus on advancing student and staff learning" (2002, p. 12).

There are four criteria within the PLDF for the principal who serves as Learner and Collaborator. Each is described in greater depth below, and strategies for building leadership capacity within each criterion complete the chapter.

- Criterion 1: Facilitates the delivery of job-embedded, ongoing, coordinated professional learning opportunities that lead to increased student achievement.
- Criterion 2: Develops internal leaders and nurtures an environment of distributed leadership, collective responsibility, and collaborative decision making.
- Criterion 3: Models reflective practice, confidence, humility, perseverance, and interest in continuous growth and lifelong learning.
- Criterion 4: Participates regularly in professional learning organizations, a community of practice, and a leadership network.

Criterion 1: Facilitates the delivery of job-embedded, ongoing, coordinated professional learning opportunities that lead to increased student achievement

Successful principals know the one thing that will make the greatest difference in student achievement: teacher quality. Building teachers' capacity, then, should be squarely at the top of any success-oriented principal's to-do list. How do principals create the structure and environment in which this happens—and happens effectively? Joyce and Showers conducted early research on transferring skills to practice and found that coaching, feedback, and collaboration, when job embedded, trumped simple training and observation (1982, p. 5).

Using an intentional coaching model, coupled with deliberate, targeted, differentiated feedback and support, can pay immense dividends (Hall & Simeral, 2008). Ultimately, the goal is to have a highly skilled, highly reflective teaching staff that works collaboratively and continues to grow and learn. When teachers are more effective, students learn more; the cause-and-effect relationship is pretty clear. Principals are in charge of establishing this culture, implementing a cohesive professional learning plan, and monitoring its impact (Reeves, 2010).

COLLABORATIVE LEADERSHIP IN ACTION

Professional development used to mean a day of droning presentations to dread. No longer is that the case at Gibsonville Elementary School in the Guildford County (North Carolina) School District. Under the guidance of principal Jessica Bohn, ongoing professional learning has become a welcome way of growing and improving. Bohn wanted to meet individual teachers' needs, since "all teachers do not learn and improve in the same way." So, with the help of her teaching staff, she created a multitiered professional learning system within her school, addressing whole-school, small-group, and individual teacher needs.

With a variety of options during early-release days, summer book studies, PLC meetings, and local/national workshops, Bohn is able to offer choice and ownership into teachers' growth programs. By sprinkling in individual coaching support, intentional walkthroughs with feedback, and structured analyses of teachers' own student data, the learning has become more relevant and job embedded. As a result, teachers feel valued, classroom instruction is improving, and student performance has grown significantly. "When I meet individual teacher needs, they're better able to engage in the difficult work of meeting individual student needs," shared Bohn. "Everyone wins."

At the district level, the implications of this criterion are also pretty clear: districts should take whatever steps are necessary to augment and facilitate the professional learning aspirations of everyone on staff and support principals in their quest to drive consistent professional learning within the building. School districts, though equipped with well-intentioned innovative approaches to improve teaching and learning, often create unintended consequences for school staff, resulting in "initiative fatigue" (Reeves, 2010). By clarifying goals and emphasizing job-embedded learning opportunities, districts can support a unifying vision for high-quality instruction and professional development.

Not surprisingly, many building leaders could use some knowledge, skill, and transfer support as well. With the changing nature of educational research and pedagogical approaches, bolstering the Lead Learners' tool belts can have a significant impact within a building. As district leaders plan professional learning for current and aspiring principals, programming should be "designed to develop and enhance the acquisition of an explicit set of knowledge, skills, and ways of thinking that mirror a school leader's responsibilities" (Pajardo, 2009, p. 132). Additionally, Pajardo's research (2009) reminds leadership development program staff that professional learning should be evaluated to determine its short-term and long-range impact.

Criterion 2: Develops internal leaders and nurtures an environment of distributed leadership, collective responsibility, and collaborative decision making

Running a school building is no easy task. No matter how dynamic, charismatic, and knowledgeable a principal is, trying to lead a school alone will prove fruitless and frustrating for everyone involved. In his seminal leadership text *Good to Great*, Jim Collins introduced us to the concept of "level 5" leadership: those whose "ambition is first and foremost for the institution, not themselves" (2001, p. 21). In that vein, cultivating and distributing leadership responsibilities throughout the school is among the level 5 leader's top priorities. From growing assistant principals to identifying teacher leaders and sharing traditional leadership duties, there is no shortage of avenues for building leadership capacity throughout a school.

> Principals who are confident and secure are more likely to nurture an atmosphere where teacher leadership can take root and thrive. These principals know that sharing leadership with teachers does not diminish their control but instead enables them to increase their impact in their buildings. In order to thrive, these principals know they must empower others (Childs-Bowen, 2006, p. 2)

The result is a staff with ownership of the process and product, momentum for key initiatives, shared decision making, broad collaboration, and increased reflective practice (Lambert, 1998).

Just like running a school, running a district is no easy task. And just like principals, dynamic, charismatic, and knowledgeable superintendents cannot do it alone. This is one of the explicit themes of this book: building leadership capacity is of the utmost importance to the success—and the very survival—of the educational institution. Coupling the continued development of principals with the professional growth of assistant principals, those aspiring to the principalship, and those who occupy the many leadership roles sprinkled throughout the system, district officials can ensure a deep pool of current and future leaders. Throughout this book are examples, strategies, and explanations that support this point. At the risk of overstating the point, we'll choose brevity: this approach is key.

COLLABORATIVE LEADERSHIP IN ACTION

As the director of professional development in the Atlanta Public Schools, coauthor Deborah Childs-Bowen sought ways to build teachers' capacity while addressing systematic professional learning needs. Her vision was to develop interdependent levels of leaders throughout the district who actively support one another's learning to achieve powerful student outcomes. One strategy she selected was to bring together the respected expert teachers in the district. Engaging mentors, accomplished content-area teachers, and those with National Board certification in conversations about their vision for adult learning and teacher leadership, Childs-Bowen led problem-solving sessions and built networks among these master educators. With reflective learning as a goal, this collection of the system's teacher leaders participated in inquiry together; codesigned and cofacilitated programs together; utilized one another as resources; and developed the confidence, voice, and authority to influence others' learning throughout the district. "For quite some time, we have looked at leadership through an anointed lens," says Childs-Bowen. "However, to make the necessary impact in education systems, it requires leadership impact at all levels."

Criterion 3: Models reflective practice, confidence, humility, perseverance, and interest in continuous growth and lifelong learning

If one were to list the characteristics of effective leaders, the adjectives would likely extend as far as the eye can see. However, as the figurehead for the school, the principal must demonstrate—in words and deeds—the core values common to the school community. Jim Collins described level 5 leaders as "quiet, humble, modest, reserved, shy, gracious, and mild-mannered" (2001, p. 27). Effective leaders speak in the language of *we* and *us*, rather than *I* and *me*.

As role models, this distinction is important. Teachers, staff, community members, business partners, visitors, and (most important) students take note of the leader's behaviors, attitudes, decisions, and dispositions. Principals, in addition to whatever other core values and morals are unique to the school community, must model the mindset and approach expected of others throughout the school. It could easily be said that the staff's attitude and the students' behavior are but reflections of the leader's image.

COLLABORATIVE LEADERSHIP IN ACTION

Sarena Jaafar, a private school principal in Pasir Mas, Kelantan, Malaysia, has embodied the role of CLO (Chief Learning Officer) in her daily practice. Her humble approach, akin to servant leadership, truly puts the needs of others at the forefront of all of her decisions. With a growing school population, an acceleration of technology use, and a shifting elementary education landscape, Jaafar must keep pace.

"Change is the only constant," she says. "I need to grow professionally to make sure I can lead my school's improvement." A vocal force in proposing professional development initiatives for her colleagues and teachers, Jaafar constantly reads, pursues advanced degrees, and talks with others to extend her learning. "I realized I can't do everything. Knowing my own limitations as a school leader makes me brave enough to admit I need to continuously learn." Rising student achievement indexes, a six-fold increase in enrollment, and burgeoning school pride reflect the leader's quest for improvement. Says Jaafar, "I'm a better leader when my staff and teachers are better at their jobs."

The unique duality of "modest and willful, humble and fearless" leadership is not confined to the building principal (Collins, 2001). School district officials must similarly model the behaviors they wish their principals to engage in, and they must take steps to nurture those characteristics in their school leaders. Leading principals, assistant principals, and future school leaders through a process of introspection, using tailored feedback from a variety of sources, can be a valuable first step. Offering collaborative professional learning opportunities to learn, practice, and refine approaches that display the agreed-upon core values helps transfer the skill into practice (Joyce & Showers, 1982). Through partnership, as well as through coaching and mentoring efforts, district leaders can support their principals in fostering these mindsets.

Criterion 4: Participates regularly in professional learning organizations, a community of practice, and a leadership network

As we mentioned in Criterion 2, running a school is impossible to do alone. Fortunately, there are thousands of other schools, almost all of them staffed with a principal, who face similar challenges with similar obstacles in similar contexts. Why not partner with them and build a learning network together? In the modern era, connecting with fellow administrators across the globe is sometimes as simple and as quick as partnering with an administrator across the street!

Online resources, chat rooms, blogs, social media, and other avenues are at our disposal, just waiting to bridge the gap between solitude and community. School principals who seek out colleagues often build lasting relationships, create mentor-mentee relationships, diversify their thinking, expand their options, and deepen their learning. All of this in addition to having an impartial, nonjudgmental, politic-free sounding board to safely suggest a course of action (or to receive feedback on a proposed action) nets the savvy principal a web of resources, confidants, experts, and peers.

COLLABORATIVE LEADERSHIP IN ACTION

As the director of staff development in the Gwinnett County (Georgia) Public Schools, DeNelle West is superbly positioned to facilitate the organization of learning networks for the district's 11,000 contracted employees. She makes the most of this opportunity, connecting educators within teams (she calls this "inner work") and between departments (referred to as "outer work") to create organic, dynamic partnerships. Bringing people together is just good practice.

In a professional network, says West, "you learn new ideas and research that may catapult your efforts to a new level." A recent focus of her department was to orchestrate collegial support of teacher leaders throughout the district who were implementing change, leading teams, and serving as mentors. By facilitating collective learning and placing candidates for a district-generated coach endorsement program into smaller cohorts, the results have been stellar: the teacher leaders are empowered, continue to learn, model best practices, and are recognized for their "grit and grace." West notes that many continue to seek one another out and seek out new collaborators to expand their ever-growing network of learners.

Principal supervisors sit in a unique position to support principals in this criterion. With access to all of the district's resources, including all of its leaders (i.e., principals, assistant principals, directors, specialists, and others), district officials can intentionally partner school principals with one another, create networks, facilitate conversations, and enhance the collaborative nature of the district's work. In addition, district influence in establishing leadership communities, when aligned to the agreed-upon mission and vision, allows for pooling resources, blending talents, sharing responsibilities, and reinforcing goals and action plans (Van Clay, Soldwedel, & Many, 2011). In this regard, fostering a collaborative culture within the leadership ranks behooves the district as much as it supports the individual (and collective) leaders.

Growing as a Learner and Collaborator: Strategies for Reflective Growth

In the following sections, we offer several strategies for building principals' leadership capacity within this role. Each provides the opportunity for the principal (Pathway One) and the district-level supervisors (Pathway Two) to clarify the work and streamline all efforts toward the long-term outcome: develop and refine reflective practices while simultaneously augmenting expertise in these criteria. Simply put, we're aiming for principals to operate in the Refinement stage as Learner and Collaborator.

The strategies we offer in Figure 6.1 are but a sampling of the many avenues to approach growth within each criterion. The strategies we have selected deliver high-leverage, universal results, and many of them include tools, templates, protocols, and forms you can find in Appendix B and online at www.ascd.org/ASCD/pdf/books/TPI2016.pdf. It is our intent to provide immediately actionable, easily implemented strategies that bridge the gap between research and application. Strategies with a support resource in Appendix B are marked with an asterisk (*).

With a thorough understanding of the role and criteria that contribute to effective instructional leadership within the role of a learner and collaborator, a good place to begin is with an honest self-assessment. Reflect on each criterion as a separate piece of your leadership puzzle. Within each criterion, we have added a brief self-assessment guide to facilitate leaders' exploration of their current thinking and technical proficiency. In the Reflective Leadership Planning Template (found in Appendix A and downloadable at www.ascd.org/ASCD/pdf/books/TPI2016.pdf), we suggest that principals (or assistant principals or aspiring principals) sit down with their supervisors/mentors/coaches and collaboratively record a narrative of their own current reality, including where they operate on the Principal's Continuum of Self-Reflection.

After scrutinizing the sample strategies that follow and collaboratively brainstorming additional strategies (with colleagues, supervisors, and others in your professional learning network), use the Reflective Leadership Planning Template

FIGURE 6.1

Principal as Learner and Collaborator Strategy Schematic

	CRITERION 1: Facilitates the delivery of job-embedded, ongoing, coordinated professional learning opportunities that lead to increased student achievement.	**CRITERION 2:** Develops internal leaders and nurtures an environment of distributed leadership, collective responsibility, and collaborative decision making.	**CRITERION 3:** Models reflective practice, confidence, humility, perseverance, and interest in continuous growth and lifelong learning.	**CRITERION 4:** Participates regularly in professional learning organizations, a community of practice, and a leadership network.
PATHWAY ONE: SCHOOL LEVEL	• Develop School-Based PD Plans Using the Six *C*s* • Use Faculty Meetings as Opportunities for Learning • Assess Prior Knowledge and Experience*	• Lead Talent Development • Take Stock of Distributed Leadership*	• Tackle a Big Challenge to Foster Perseverance • Be a Role Model*	• Conduct Personal Action Research* • Boomerang
PATHWAY TWO: DISTRICT LEVEL	• Analyze the Impact of PD* • Assess Organizational Support for Professional Learning* • Address Initiative Fatigue	• Select Teacher Leaders Strategically • Select Mentor Principals*	• Highlight the Human Element* • Model the Way to Continuous Improvement	• Create Principal Communities of Practice • Read and Lead*

Note: Strategies with an asterisk (*) include a tool/template/protocol/form in Appendix B.

to document the powerful steps you will take to develop your (or your principal's) growth as a reflective learner and collaborator. There is great strength in the dialogue, collaboration, and partnership in this goal-setting endeavor; utilize the resources at your disposal to create and refine a clear, focused, reflection-oriented plan.

Criterion 1

Guiding Question: How can we all continue to learn and grow as professionals?

Theory of Action: The more we learn, the more effective we will be, and learning must be enmeshed in our work on a daily basis (Hall & Simeral, 2008; Joyce & Showers, 1982). If the principal facilitates the delivery of job-embedded, ongoing professional learning opportunities (for self and staff) that are based on mission, vision, and established site needs and that focus on results, then teaching and learning will improve for both staff and students.

In Figure 6.2, the Principal's Continuum of Self-Reflection describes the depth of thinking related to leadership actions in this criterion. To the right of each stage is the focus behavior for developing reflective capacity within the criterion. Refer to the Reflective Cycle (Figure 2.3, p. 17) and the focused reflective questions (Figure 2.4, p. 22) for more guidance.

FIGURE 6.2

P-CSR: *Learner and Collaborator Criterion 1*

UNAWARE STAGE	BUILD AWARENESS	CONSCIOUS STAGE	PLAN INTENTIONALLY	ACTION STAGE	ACCURATELY ASSESS IMPACT	REFINEMENT STAGE	BECOME RESPONSIVE
Tends to professional development as an add-on service for staff.		Provides resources in support of professional development endeavors that may or may not relate to mission and vision.		Arranges professional development opportunities for staff that support the mission, vision, and currently assessed site needs.		Facilitates the delivery of job-embedded, ongoing professional learning opportunities for self and staff, based on mission, vision, and established site needs, that focus on results.	

Pathway One: School Level

Develop School-Based PD Plans Using the Six Cs*

Professional development endeavors, no matter how well intentioned, will only be as effective as they are embraced by the learner. Principals and building leaders creating school-based professional development plans must make sure the plan includes the components of effective professional development. A checklist that helps to determine if the six Cs—connected, collaborative, customized, coordinated, comprehensive, and consistent—are in place will support planning, implementation, monitoring, and refinement. Leadership teams can make sure that the checklist is used by teacher leaders and others in the building responsible for ongoing professional learning. We have included the checklist Developing School-Based PD Plans Using the Six Cs for your immediate reference (Appendix B.37).

Use Faculty Meetings as Opportunities for Learning

Principals leading the way in job-embedded professional learning often start with redesigning the most consistent time they have with the instructional staff—their faculty meetings. Include action steps in the faculty meeting redesign that answer the following questions: What are some critical learning needs within our building that we could address during this precious time together? How will I ensure that the professional learning experiences are applicable to the entire staff? How will I engage different staff members in facilitation, collaboration, and leadership? How will I address resistant staff members? How will I make sure the experience is differentiated to meet teacher and staff needs? How will I extend redesigned faculty meetings to other staff meetings in the school so that meetings as professional learning opportunities become part of the school culture? In what alternative ways will I share important administrative information that staff members are accustomed to receiving at faculty meetings? By addressing these questions in advance, principals can effectively reallocate their time together to build collective capacity.

Assess Prior Knowledge and Experience*

Principals who promote job-embedded professional learning also make sure that differentiating the experiences is an expectation. Principals and others in the building responsible for professional learning can make sure they include participant preassessments as an integral part of designing job-embedded experiences. Include questions that determine current knowledge and experience related to the topic, learning preferences, and sharing and collaboration preferences. Use the results to inform PLC work as well as individualized professional learning plans for teachers. By using the Assessing Prior Knowledge and Learning Preferences tool (Appendix B.38), principals can help staff craft a learning plan to move toward Point B—after identifying their current Point A.

Pathway Two: District Level

Analyze the Impact of PD*

Some of the "greatest" professional development experiences have yielded very little impact on the teachers who participated in them or on the students who were ultimately supposed to have benefited. Why? Lack of a model for determining the success of implementation and effect. District-level leaders who support principal leadership development must ensure that principals know why and how to gather relevant evidence in their buildings. Supervisors, mentors, and coaches can have principals review a PD plan from the previous year or a draft of their current PD plan with a focus on the following questions: What do we want to know or learn, and how will we assess whether we learned it? How will we know when we have adequately answered our driving questions? What sources, processes, or documentation could we use to gather evidence of our learning? By whom, to whom, when, and how will we report professional learning impact? In the end, the question that drives this process is this: How will we know if this professional learning has led to increases in student outputs? The Evaluating PD Impact tool (Appendix B.39) provides a framework for principal teams and their supervisors to analyze school-based PD efforts.

Assess Organizational Support for Professional Learning*

Before engaging in the facilitation and delivery of principal leadership development, assess the current state of your principals' professional learning experiences. Does the district's professional learning plan for leaders (current and future) and/or instructional staff meet the standard of the six Cs? Complete a self-assessment focusing on the support the district provides for principal leadership development and school-based professional development. Use the results to enhance district leadership development and school-based PD support. In Appendix B.40, we have provided a tool to help district leaders begin this process.

Address Initiative Fatigue

The practice of shifting from one great idea to the next, without giving the first initiative time to become implemented, refined, and deeply ingrained into systematic practice, leads to a phenomenon called "initiative fatigue" (Reeves, 2010). This is when personnel (teachers and administrators, or those responsible for carrying out the plans) begin to resist new ideas. District leaders can support principals in taking steps to eliminate initiative fatigue at the school level prior to planning school-based job-embedded professional learning. Have principals gather in small groups based on school feeder patterns. Facilitate a review and examination of district and school initiatives in order to find common elements. Then create a visual that shows how those initiatives are connected. Make sure feeder-pattern principals add any additional school-based initiatives to the visual before distributing it at their schools. This strategy can also be used as a precursor to selective abandonment of initiatives that are no longer needed.

Criterion 2

Guiding Question: How can we build and share leadership throughout the school?
Theory of Action: Running an educational organization alone is counterproductive. Sharing leadership roles and building leadership capacity throughout the ranks will affect the entire school environment in a positive manner (Lambert, 1998, 2003).

If the principal develops internal leaders and nurtures a culturally responsive environment of shared ownership and decision making, then the school will be positioned for greater long-term success.

In Figure 6.3, the Principal's Continuum of Self-Reflection describes the depth of thinking related to leadership actions in this criterion. To the right of each stage is the focus behavior for developing reflective capacity within the criterion. Refer to the Reflective Cycle (Figure 2.3, p. 17) and the focused reflective questions (Figure 2.4, p. 22) for more guidance.

FIGURE 6.3

P-CSR: *Learner and Collaborator Criterion 2*

UNAWARE STAGE	BUILD AWARENESS	CONSCIOUS STAGE	PLAN INTENTIONALLY	ACTION STAGE	ACCURATELY ASSESS IMPACT	REFINEMENT STAGE	BECOME RESPONSIVE
Accepts hierarchical structures and follows established decision-making processes.		Incorporates some shared decision-making practices and works within the established leadership structures.		Provides opportunities for leaders to emerge through collaborative decision-making structures.		Develops internal leaders and nurtures a culturally responsive environment of shared ownership and decision making.	

Pathway One: School Level

Lead Talent Development

According to the Center for Public Education, because of the challenges and demands of leading a school and because principals' tenure averages just three or four years in a school, talent acquisition and development are key responsibilities of building leaders (Hull, 2012). Principals must engage assistant principals in a variety of opportunities and experiences that prepare them for building leadership, since they're "next in line." This variety also saves assistant principals from being pigeonholed into one type of on-the-job learning role—such as disciplinarian—devoid of instructional leadership experiences. Establish clarity of authority and decision making for people assuming new roles, and abide by these agreements as they support the growth of other leaders across the school. These same types of practices then extend to department or grade-level chairs, coaches, classroom teachers, and ultimately students. In this way, principals can recognize the value and obligation they have to share in developing leadership capacity with the school.

Take Stock of Distributed Leadership*

Effectively distributing leadership allows principals to build leadership capacity among the staff while reallocating time and energy to the responsibilities unique to the principalship. Engaging in personal reflection about opportunities and obstacles to distributing leadership among staff is important for principals to inform their planning. During reflection, list current opportunities for other staff to assume some responsibility or partner to distribute the leadership. Committees, action teams, programs, professional learning efforts, and other events can provide excellent opportunities for aspiring leaders to stretch their leadership wings. Also, list opportunities for distributed leadership that aren't currently in place along with potential obstacles to moving forward. With a critical friend, colleague, or members of the established leadership team, exchange reflections, engage in dialogue, and plan the next steps to distribute those leadership responsibilities. Use the Taking Stock of Distributed Leadership tool (Appendix B.41) to guide these reflections.

Pathway Two: District Level

Select Teacher Leaders Strategically

Many teachers have leadership abilities and aspirations, and accessing these assets is of clear benefit to the district. District leaders can support principals in identifying teacher leaders by making sure there is districtwide criteria for teacher leaders in place and by developing an application and selection process that is transparent to all. A principal leadership development meeting should be set aside each year to engage in small-group peer review of criteria and applications aligned to district needs and focus areas. After teacher leaders are identified and selected, it is also incumbent on the district to provide opportunities for their continued growth and development as leaders. Ensuring that there are committees, task forces, advisory panels, peer coaching/mentoring programs, and other structures in place will enable teacher leaders to grow their leadership capacity for years to come.

Select Mentor Principals*

Principal supervisors serve many roles and are responsible for developing the talent of future and current leaders. To expand leadership capacities of experienced principals, and to create a web of interconnected support system for school leaders, supervisors can establish a formal principal mentoring program. The mentors, selected from a pool of accomplished principals, assist in the development of novice and aspiring principals across the district. Through a selection process (which includes questions such as those in the Principal Mentor Selection Tool found in Appendix B.42), choose mentors who are knowledgeable of curriculum, assessment, and instructional practices; are current in their field; and are effective communicators. Because mentors serve as role models, choose individuals who possess other positive qualities (i.e., they are professional, supportive, caring, and respectful) (Pajardo, 2009).

Criterion 3

Guiding Question: How can I model the traits that we value?

Theory of Action: The way a principal behaves can have a ripple effect throughout a school community. Pete Hall writes, "The principal must model not perfection, but the pursuit of it" (2011, p. 14). If the principal models reflective practice, confidence, humility, perseverance, and interest in continuous growth and lifelong learning, then the entire school community will reflect those characteristics.

In Figure 6.4, the Principal's Continuum of Self-Reflection describes the depth of thinking related to leadership actions in this criterion. To the right of each stage is the focus behavior for developing reflective capacity within the criterion. Refer to the Reflective Cycle (Figure 2.3, p. 17) and the focused reflective questions (Figure 2.4, p. 22) for more guidance.

FIGURE 6.4

P-CSR: *Learner and Collaborator Criterion 3*

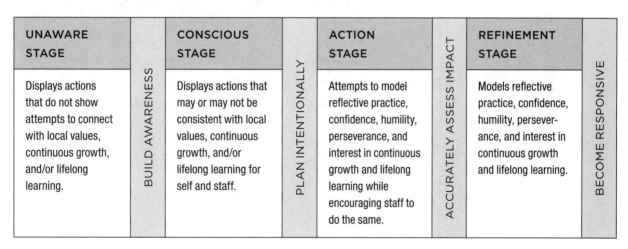

UNAWARE STAGE	BUILD AWARENESS	CONSCIOUS STAGE	PLAN INTENTIONALLY	ACTION STAGE	ACCURATELY ASSESS IMPACT	REFINEMENT STAGE	BECOME RESPONSIVE
Displays actions that do not show attempts to connect with local values, continuous growth, and/or lifelong learning.		Displays actions that may or may not be consistent with local values, continuous growth, and/or lifelong learning for self and staff.		Attempts to model reflective practice, confidence, humility, perseverance, and interest in continuous growth and lifelong learning while encouraging staff to do the same.		Models reflective practice, confidence, humility, perseverance, and interest in continuous growth and lifelong learning.	

Pathway One: School Level

Tackle a Big Challenge to Foster Perseverance

Principals focused on perseverance can demonstrate it by leading the staff in taking on a persistent schoolwide challenge and finding ways to address it. At the beginning of the year, facilitate a faculty meeting in which the staff comes to consensus on the biggest student learning or attitude challenge. Once it's identified, have grade-level, team, or department groups work together to "unpack" student and teacher factors that contribute to the challenge. Next, teams work together to develop action steps they will take each semester. Designate faculty meetings during the semester where groups will share their progress and evidence. At the end of the year, take another look at the challenge to shine a light on the rewards of persevering as a team. If the staff does not make the headway expected or desired, that provides an additional opportunity to foster resilience and persistence. Continue the work and brainstorm new strategies, approaches, or ideas for conquering this confounding challenge.

Be a Role Model*

As the figurehead of the school, the principal is the ultimate role model—for the staff, student body, and entire school community. Principals must embrace that reality and *live* it by operating in accord with the school community's accepted values in every interaction, conversation, and appearance, even during "unofficial sightings" (e.g., in the audience at a local sporting event or restaurant). Indeed, principals successful in this regard are stout of character and consistent; they also are keenly aware of the community's core values.

Some valuable approaches in the school environment include modeling openness to new ideas and continuous learning. Principals model this mindset by demonstrating an ability to listen, analyze, and persist in the face of challenges. In addition, principals model a sense of personal efficacy and communicate their expectations to students and adults. They view challenges as an opportunity to learn by selecting a problem-solving protocol for use schoolwide. (We offer a familiar example with the Consultancy Protocol, found in Appendix B.18.) Principals can further develop a culture of efficacy by including the integration of noncognitive factors for student success, such as confidence, grit, and humility, into school, grade-level, and department plans and practices.

Pathway Two: District Level

Highlight the Human Element*

Education is a people business, and effective principals tend to have superb interpersonal skills. Interestingly, most principal evaluations barely touch on the important human factors that make principals successful leaders. Therefore, in addition to reflective practices, principal leadership development programs must include support in the areas of confidence building, perseverance, and engagement. District leaders should develop look-fors and how-to guides, such as those we have provided in the Human Side of the Principalship Matrix (Appendix B.43), for use by supervisors, coaches, and mentors so principals will have examples of how to demonstrate these important human behaviors in their everyday responsibilities.

Model the Way to Continuous Improvement

District officials can show their own humility and commitment to continuous growth by completing the self-assessment guides at the end of Chapters 3–6 from the perspective of their own role. Even though they were written with principals in mind, they are still appropriate for principal supervisors. Include reflections and goals related to a selected self-assessment criterion at each touch-base meeting with principals. This open and honest focus on leadership growth demonstrates a commitment to lifelong learning, strengthens the partnership, and contributes to an increase in effectiveness within the leadership role.

Criterion 4

Guiding Question: How can I collaborate with others and continue to grow professionally?

Theory of Action: The principalship can be a lonely position (Rooney, 2000). Partnering with other leaders produces many mutually beneficial results, including a feeling of partnership on the journey. If the principal participates regularly in a community of practice, leadership network, and professional learning organization(s), then the power of the collective will support the individual, leading to sustained school improvement.

In Figure 6.5, the Principal's Continuum of Self-Reflection describes the depth of thinking related to leadership actions in this criterion. To the right of each stage is the focus behavior for developing reflective capacity within the criterion. Refer to the Reflective Cycle (Figure 2.3, p. 17) and the focused reflective questions (Figure 2.4, p. 22) for more guidance.

Pathway One: School Level

Conduct Personal Action Research*

Every school site is different and presents challenges unique to its particular context. Principals can take strides toward figuring out how to solve a specific problem of practice in their schools by developing a personal action research project using these steps: (1) Determine the action research question, such as "Why are so many of our African American and Latino families not participating in the after-hours events the school sponsors?" (2) Decide on strategies or practices that will be tried out to address

FIGURE 6.5

P-CSR: *Learner and Collaborator Criterion 4*

UNAWARE STAGE	BUILD AWARENESS	CONSCIOUS STAGE	PLAN INTENTIONALLY	ACTION STAGE	ACCURATELY ASSESS IMPACT	REFINEMENT STAGE	BECOME RESPONSIVE
Works independently, without seeking support from a Community of Practice or professional learning organization.		Considers membership in a Community of Practice or professional organization on occasion.		Accesses colleagues through a Community of Practice, leadership network, or professional learning organization.		Participates regularly in a Community of Practice, leadership network, and professional learning organization(s).	

the problem of practice, such as scheduling one of the events at a neighborhood church or community center or partnering with one of the high school student organizations to provide free child care for an event scheduled at night. (3) As the strategies are implemented, gather data and document the results, noting trends and outliers. (4) Determine which strategies or practices provided the most effective solution to the problem of practice. Use the Action Research Planning Template (Appendix B.44) to plan your work and monitor your progress. For added benefits, select a colleague with whom you can work on the project and share the journey.

Boomerang

Principals build their communities of practice by seeking out colleagues with similar assignments, traits, personalities, or skills. Often, principals who seek ongoing growth and continuous improvement gravitate toward other principals who innovate and share. These networks operate with the informal agreement that sharing is a reciprocal process—a certain quid pro quo—that results in a boomerang effect. These exchanges happen formally, during official principals' meetings or other scheduled gatherings, as well as intermittently through phone calls, texts, e-mails, and face-to-face connections. When these connections occur, each principal brings a problem of practice that is supported through inquiry, collaboration, observation, feedback loops, and coaching to affect teaching, learning, and leadership in their schools.

Pathway Two: District Level

Create Principal Communities of Practice

Time spent with principals in a structured meeting setting is a precious commodity—akin to a principal bringing together all staff at a faculty meeting. Changing traditional principal meetings into Community of Practice meetings is a strategy that district supervisors will find effective in building leadership capacity. Based on the results of the self-assessment guides principals will complete at the end of Chapters 3–6, have each principal select two to three Communities of Practice (small teams of professionals who work collaboratively and interdependently to address issues, solve problems, and support one another) they will work with during the school year. Provide time for these communities to collaborate and problem solve at each meeting, and provide private virtual collaboration tools/space to support ongoing collaboration. By allocating time and providing direction for this practice, principals may be motivated to seek out other professional contacts and networks beyond the confines of their own district—online, through social media, or via membership with a professional organization.

Read and Lead*

Continuous improvement stems from an unyielding desire to know more, do more, and perform at a higher level. Ellie Drago-Severson explains, "Just as it is important to provide contexts for teachers to engage in collegial inquiry, so too is it important for principals" (2004, p. 6). District officials and principal supervisors can issue a challenge to principals in their jurisdiction (i.e., network/level/cluster/administrative area) to read at least six professional books in one school year. Start with having each principal read two books independently. Post pictures in the central office, on the website, or on a social media channel showing principals and principal supervisors "reading and leading." Discuss the effect these texts have on each principal's leadership decisions, knowledge, or perspective.

Move to reading and discussing two books with each school's administrative team. Progress to reading and discussing two books in an administrators-as-readers group with colleagues in feeder-school patterns, networks, or administrative regions. Use the Reflections on Professional Reading template (Appendix B.45) to capture reflections as principals "read and lead."

Where to Start

Gaining a comprehensive understanding of the principal's role as learner and collaborator is one thing; synthesizing the complex bank of strategies into the nuanced context of a particular school or district is another thing altogether. Before we offer a suggested course of action, let us be clear: it is neither our intent nor our expectation that school or district leaders take the strategies discussed in this chapter as "marching orders," proceeding through the list and checking them off when "complete." Rather, they are options for growing as a learner and collaborator while simultaneously developing as a reflective practitioner.

In the following section (see Figure 6.6), we have included a self-assessment guide to help provide clarity and direction for your next steps. Though this can be used as a self-directed growth tool, it is preferable to utilize it collaboratively—with peers, colleagues, and supervisors—in order to extract the maximum benefit. For principal supervisors and district officials, this guide can be particularly useful when sitting down with building leaders to set goals, analyze performance, and create a plan to build leadership capacity within the role of Learner and Collaborator.

Directions for the Self-Assessment Guide

1. Review the stages of the Principal's Continuum of Self-Reflection (P-CSR) along each criterion.
2. Highlight words or phrases and jot down notes regarding your reflective tendencies and professional practice within each criterion.
3. Depending on the stage of the P-CSR at which you believe you are operating, identify the action from the Reflective Cycle that requires your focus.
    a. If you are operating in the Unaware stage, your goal is to build awareness.
    b. If you are operating in the Conscious stage, your goal is to plan intentionally.
    c. If you are operating in the Action stage, your goal is to assess impact.
    d. If you are operating in the Refinement stage, your goal is to become responsive.
4. Select a strategy from either Pathway One (school level) or Pathway Two (district level) that will help you address this criterion.
5. After completing this task for all four criteria within the principal's role as Learner and Collaborator, collaboratively select the one key criterion on which you are ready to focus.
6. Use the Reflective Leadership Planning Template (Appendix A) to create a thorough, robust plan for growing as a learner and collaborator while simultaneously developing as a reflective practitioner.

FIGURE 6.6

Principal as Learner and Collaborator Self-Assessment Guide

	UNAWARE STAGE	CONSCIOUS STAGE	ACTION STAGE	REFINEMENT STAGE
CRITERION 1: Facilitates the delivery of job-embedded, ongoing, coordinated professional learning opportunities that lead to increased student achievement.	Tends to professional development as an add-on service for staff.	Provides resources in support of professional development endeavors that may or may not relate to mission and vision.	Arranges professional development opportunities for staff that support the mission, vision, and currently assessed site needs.	Facilitates the delivery of job-embedded, ongoing professional learning opportunities for self and staff, based on mission, vision, and established site needs, that focus on results.

1. Why do you feel this stage is an accurate representation of your thinking about this criterion?

2. Which action from the Reflective Cycle requires your focus in order to grow as a reflective practitioner? (See Figure 2.3 for guidance.)
   Build Awareness   Plan Intentionally   Accurately Assess Progress   Be Responsive

3. Which strategy listed under Criterion 1 might best support your growth as you take action?

	UNAWARE STAGE	CONSCIOUS STAGE	ACTION STAGE	REFINEMENT STAGE
CRITERION 2: Develops internal leaders and nurtures an environment of distributed leadership, collective responsibility, and collaborative decision making.	Accepts hierarchical structures and follows established decision-making processes.	Incorporates some shared decision-making practices and works within the established leadership structures.	Provides opportunities for leaders to emerge through collaborative decision-making structures.	Develops internal leaders and nurtures a culturally responsive environment of shared ownership and decision making.

1. Why do you feel this stage is an accurate representation of your thinking about this criterion?

2. Which action from the Reflective Cycle requires your focus in order to grow as a reflective practitioner? (See Figure 2.3 for guidance.)
   Build Awareness   Plan Intentionally   Accurately Assess Progress   Be Responsive

3. Which strategy listed under Criterion 2 might best support your growth as you take action?

Continued

FIGURE 6.6

Principal as Learner and Collaborator Self-Assessment Guide (continued)

	UNAWARE STAGE	CONSCIOUS STAGE	ACTION STAGE	REFINEMENT STAGE
CRITERION 3: Models reflective practice, confidence, humility, perseverance, and interest in continuous growth and lifelong learning.	Displays actions that do not show attempts to connect with local values, continuous growth, and/or lifelong learning.	Displays actions that may or may not be consistent with local values, continuous growth, and/or lifelong learning for self and staff.	Attempts to model reflective practice, confidence, humility, perseverance, and interest in continuous growth and lifelong learning while encouraging staff to do the same.	Models reflective practice, confidence, humility, perseverance, and interest in continuous growth and lifelong learning.

1. Why do you feel this stage is an accurate representation of your thinking about this criterion?

2. Which action from the Reflective Cycle requires your focus in order to grow as a reflective practitioner? (See Figure 2.3 for guidance.)

   Build Awareness   Plan Intentionally   Accurately Assess Progress   Be Responsive

3. Which strategy listed under Criterion 3 might best support your growth as you take action?

	UNAWARE STAGE	CONSCIOUS STAGE	ACTION STAGE	REFINEMENT STAGE
CRITERION 4: Participates regularly in professional learning organizations, a Community of Practice, and a leadership network.	Works independently, without seeking support from a Community of Practice or professional learning organization.	Considers membership in a Community of Practice or professional organization on occasion.	Accesses colleagues through a Community of Practice, leadership network, or professional learning organization.	Participates regularly in a Community of Practice, leadership network, and professional learning organization(s).

1. Why do you feel this stage is an accurate representation of your thinking about this criterion?

2. Which action from the Reflective Cycle requires your focus in order to grow as a reflective practitioner? (See Figure 2.3 for guidance.)

   Build Awareness   Plan Intentionally   Accurately Assess Progress   Be Responsive

3. Which strategy listed under Criterion 4 might best support your growth as you take action?

CHAPTER 7
Reflective Leadership Awaits

"Risk more than others think is safe, care more than others think is wise, dream more than others think is practical, expect more than others think is possible." —Cadet maxim

In the Introduction to Part II of this book, we encouraged you to be creative, keep an open mind, and embrace the possibilities that are contained herein. Embedded within this request are two key elements: possibility and intentionality.

> **Possibility:** Progressive and future-oriented people talk often of their goals, dreams, and what may come, creating vision boards, mapping the future, and considering possibilities. These folks don't just play it safe by simply accepting what *is*; they live with a strategic hope of what *could be,* and they act upon that vision.

> **Intentionality:** Possibilities only become realities when they are appropriately acted upon. Effective leaders embrace this fact and perform with intentionality. Intentionality suggests a consciousness of the current state—as well as a vision for future possibilities—and indicates a leader's willingness to enact a game plan for moving from here to there.

Leadership Matters

For you to lead effectively and grow the leadership of others, you need to harness the wonderful possibilities around you and conduct your leadership development efforts with great intentionality. Leadership and leadership development are both individual and collective in nature. Effective instructional leaders embrace the personal responsibility for their own development, such as using this book and its strategies, and they recognize that certain individuals have a readiness to lead, so they guide and develop aspiring leaders. At the same time, leadership is collective, hence the expression "The power of the whole is greater than the sum of its parts." It is essential to include aspects of collaborative, systemic leadership development. It does not do the education field justice to simply develop beacons of light or a shining star. Stars burn out, so we must repopulate the field with new, more, and even brighter stars.

In others words, how we view possibilities, how we act consciously and intentionally, how individual leaders hold themselves to high-quality leadership standards and actions, and how we join collectively to grow the leadership capacity of others *matters*! What we *do* matters. If you are willing to invest your time, your efforts, and your mental energy into the high-leverage strategies within this book, the results can have a profound impact on your instructional leadership practices, which will lead to powerful teaching throughout your schools and districts and to robust learning for all students under your care.

When you accepted your position (regardless of what role you occupy), you knowingly or unknowingly accepted the responsibility for the roles outlined in this book: Visionary, Instructional Leader, Engager, and Learner and Collaborator.

- You likely made a promise to support high levels of learning for every student. This is your vision. Where are you now, and where are you headed next?
- You likely pledged to serve as an instructional leader to ensure powerful teaching and learning are the norm. Where are you now, and where are you headed next?
- You likely vowed to positively and significantly influence the school and school community to achieve this goal. Where are you now, and where are you headed next?
- Along the way, you have likely engaged in learning and collaborating with others. Where are you now, and where are you headed next?

Each of these roles is inextricably linked to the others, a diverse and interdependent web that together defines the key elements of instructional leadership. Growing as an instructional leader is complex, challenging, and dynamic work; yet at the same time, it is understandable, achievable, and meaningful. Our 21st century students and teachers deserve nothing less than 21st century leadership.

Final Thoughts from the Authors

This book came to life through a team of accomplished leaders who had never worked together as a team and who banded together to achieve a goal for which we were all very passionate. In pursuing that goal, we checked our egos, titles, past successes, and past disappointments at the door. We led and were willing to follow. We played to our strengths and were willing to take risks in unfamiliar areas. We encouraged one another, shared candid feedback, learned new approaches, reflected, and laughed along the way. In times of doubt and uncertainty, we revisited, restated, and reemphasized our vision, thereby renewing our passion.

What we did in writing this book exemplifies the power of collaboration and mirrors the leadership work of school and district teams. You have read, reflected, and set leadership goals related to the contents of this book; we also encourage you to find a team of other leaders with whom you can learn and work. We are positive that your time, progress, and results will be as meaningful as our collaborative journey in writing this book.

APPENDIX A

Reflective Leadership
Planning Template

Name:_____   School:_____

Position:_____   Date:_____

Role:_____

Specific category of focus: _____

Rationale for this focus/Description of current reality/performance:

_____

_____

Stage on the Principal's Continuum of Self-Reflection where leader is currently operating:

_____

_____

Statement of Goal (blending Reflective focus with Leadership actions):

_____

_____

How will we measure progress, success, and completion of the goal (what evidence will determine our effectiveness)?

_____

_____

List the action steps that will move us toward our goal:	What is the time-frame for accomplishing these action steps?	What support will we need to make this progress?	Who will provide that support?

APPENDIX B

Strategies for Reflective Growth

APPENDIX B.1: PREPARING AN ELEVATOR SPEECH

STEP 1:

To prepare an effective elevator speech, write your answers to the prompts below (in as many words, sentences, or paragraphs as you would like):

1. **What's your why?** This is your opportunity to "hook" your conversation partner, often with an emotional connection. A statement such as "Did you know one in three students drops out before graduating high school? Our high school is committed to a 'zero out of three' campaign" beats "I am the principal of Townsend High School. Go Lions!" any day.

2. **How is this vision distinctive?** There are many schools vying for the same resources. Why is yours special? What data can you use to highlight your school's accomplishments, history, or special characteristics? Often, folks want to connect with a school, district, or visionary idea that is unique, memorable, special, and something different.

3. **How does this benefit stakeholders?** Knowing your audience and formatting this third point can work wonders: Why would an organization want to donate to the cause? Why would a candidate want to teach at your school? Why should a family become interested in moving into your school's attendance zone? "What's in it for me?" Include a brief answer to these questions to capture your audience and to help them "see" themselves as viable partners.

4. **Where can people go for more information? And what might you need from them that is unique** Carry business cards with you with the school's website, the address to the PTA blog, your Twitter handle, key email addresses and phone numbers, and any other avenue for providing access to additional information. If you don't have a card, end with a cheerful, "Look us up on Facebook at Townsend High School!" Sharing information is helpful, however, identifying something that is needed from the listener is an important leave-behind to realize the school vision. This aspect generates commitment from the listener to be in partnership in realizing the vision.

STEP 2:

Reread your responses and pare them down to the most important information. Rewrite your responses in one to two sentences each. Brevity counts.

STEP 3:

Read them together—aloud—to make sure they flow. If it takes more than 120 seconds (2 minutes) to recite, you'll have to revise more.

STEP 4:

Practice, practice, practice. Practice in the mirror, practice with a spouse or friend, and practice with a professional colleague.

STEP 5:

Invite your administrative team, teachers, other staff, and other stakeholder leaders for feedback to refine the elevator speech as necessary. Encourage them to follow suit—the more people out there conveying the message in a passionate, articulate manner, the better for the school and its students.

From P. Hall, D. Childs-Bowen, A. Cunningham-Morris, P. Pajardo, & A. Simeral, *The Principal Influence: A Framework for Developing Leadership Capacity in Principals* (Alexandria, VA: ASCD, 2016). © 2016 ASCD.

APPENDIX B.2: CUSTOMIZED STRATEGIC COMMUNICATION PLAN

PURPOSE: This frame helps school leaders create a strategic plan for reaching each and all of their varied constituents on an ongoing, intentional basis.

STEP 1: In the spaces provided, jot down some of the vehicles you are familiar with, adding to the list we have already provided, and see whether your school or district is reaching all audience segments.

STEP 2: Individually read the short article "Say it with Social Media," by Patrick Larkin, in *Educational Leadership 72* (April 2015): 66–69, to generate even more ideas.

STEP 3: After discussing the vehicles you use now, examine the accompanying list for additional ideas. Add any great ideas from your group to the attached list and use the list as a guide for your school, grade-level, or departmental communication efforts.

AUDIENCES	VEHICLES
Students	Welcome packets Homework notebooks Instagram posts _____ _____ _____
Parents and families	Parent resource rooms Parent education workshops E-mail listservers for notices and news _____ _____ _____
Citizens and retired people	Special promotions School volunteer and mentor programs Facebook friends _____ _____ _____
School employees	School board recognitions Internal bulletins Twitter feed _____ _____ _____

Continued

APPENDIX B.2: CUSTOMIZED STRATEGIC COMMUNICATION PLAN
(CONTINUED)

Opinion leaders and key communicators	Civic and religious group meetings Personal letters and handwritten notes Phone trees for issues management _____ _____ _____
Others	Program brochures News releases School website updates _____ _____ _____

From P. Hall, D. Childs-Bowen, A. Cunningham-Morris, P. Pajardo, & A. Simeral, *The Principal Influence: A Framework for Developing Leadership Capacity in Principals* (Alexandria, VA: ASCD, 2016). © 2016 ASCD. Adapted and reprinted from p. 52 of A. Meek, R. Champion, & K. Dyer, *Guide for Instructional Leaders, Guide 3* (Alexandria, VA: ASCD, 2004).

APPENDIX B.3: TRIAD PROTOCOL

PURPOSE: This protocol is quite useful for peers to give and receive feedback on a "problem of practice" or a work-in-progress—for example, revising curriculum, constructing assessments, addressing concerns, clarifying questions, or developing policies.

PRELIMINARY STEP—FORMING GROUPS
(about 5 minutes)

1. Have people form small groups of three (hence "triad").

2. Have participants decide who will be A, B, and C in their triad.

STEP 1
(about 15 minutes)

1. Participant A serves as the presenter, describing an aspect of professional practice that is currently presenting a problem or challenge.

2. Participant B serves as the discussant, building on what participant A is saying with a comment, question, example, or detail.

3. Participant C is the observer, listening quietly, saying nothing, and taking notes.

4. After A and B have talked, C summarizes what they have said, adds comments, and presents some conclusions.

STEP 2
(about 15 minutes)

Step 1 is repeated, with the presenter, discussant, and observer switching places.

STEP 3
(about 15 minutes)

Step 2 is repeated, with the presenter, discussant, and observer switching places once more.

REFLECTIONS & DEBRIEFING
(about 10 minutes)

All participants discuss their takeaways from the feedback-rich discussion. They address such questions as:

1. What questions have you had answered during this process?

2. What questions do you still have?

3. What is your next step?

4. How will you follow up or monitor progress as you proceed?

From P. Hall, D. Childs-Bowen, A. Cunningham-Morris, P. Pajardo, & A. Simeral, *The Principal Influence: A Framework for Developing Leadership Capacity in Principals* (Alexandria, VA: ASCD, 2016). © 2016 ASCD. Adapted and reprinted from p. 60 of L. Easton, *Protocols for professional learning* (Alexandria, VA: ASCD, 2009).

APPENDIX B.4: STAKEHOLDER VISION AND TRANSITION PROCESS

PURPOSE: The data collected through this process informs the district's plan in assigning a new principal to the building. The newly hired principal is provided guidance regarding expectations for the abandonment or continuation of work toward the school community's vision. This transparency will help guide new leaders and enhance stakeholder buy-in during the transition period.

A *Stakeholder Vision and Transition Process* includes the following components:

1. Identify target stakeholder groups and collect feedback.

2. Analyze data, including teachers and school-based leaders.

3. Communicate with the school community throughout the process.

4. Consider internal and external candidates, ensuring the maintenance or reestablishment of a collective vision.

FOCUS: Areas of focus for feedback related to vision:

- Budget priorities
- Professional development practices
- Teacher leadership
- Parent involvement
- Feedback practices
- Student engagement and responsibility
- Teaching assignments
- Instructional feedback
- Expectations, structures, and support for instruction and learning
- Safety, climate, and culture
- School improvement planning
- Collaboration
- Other:_____
- Other:_____

FORMAT: Survey all invested stakeholders to get a pulse of the community's commitment to the current vision through:

- Community forums
- Online questionnaires
- Focus groups
- Designated meetings
- Other:_____

FOLLOW-UP: The new building leader, working collaboratively with district supervisors and community stakeholders, can analyze these data to create a transition plan that addresses uniquely held nuances associated with these categories and support those that yielded positive results. At the same time, they can eliminate any practices, programs, and structures that have not yielded results.

From P. Hall, D. Childs-Bowen, A. Cunningham-Morris, P. Pajardo, & A. Simeral, *The Principal Influence: A Framework for Developing Leadership Capacity in Principals* (Alexandria, VA: ASCD, 2016). © 2016 ASCD.

APPENDIX B.5: AUDITING OUR RESOURCES

DIRECTIONS: This tool can serve as a guide for principals and stakeholders in conducting quarterly resource audits—intentional analyses of expenditures (including human capital, time, and finances)—to stay on track and act with transparency. Use this form for each of the goals in your School Improvement Plan to determine the efficiency of your utilization of resources, to guide decision making, or to streamline the budgeting process.

WHICH SIP GOAL IS THE FOCUS OF THIS AUDIT?	
What resources are necessary to meet this goal? • Human capital • Time • Finances	
What resources are allocated toward this goal? • Human capital • Time • Finances	
Has the allocation of resources increased, decreased, or stayed the same in the last few years for this goal? • Human capital • Time • Finances	
What additional resources are available to support the attainment of this goal? • Human capital • Time • Finances	
What adjustments or contingency plans can we enact to meet this SIP goal this year?	
Other notes regarding this goal and available/utilized resources:	

APPENDIX B.6: DATA-DRIVEN DIALOGUE STANDARD PROTOCOL

Cohort/Team:_____   School/Principal/Teacher:_____

Date:_____   Assessment:_____

What is the purpose of this data inquiry?_____

_____

DIRECTIONS: Use this Data-Driven Dialogue (DDD) protocol to guide the investigation, analysis, and action planning around an assessment question. This DDD is useful for individual teachers, teams or departments, school-level views, and districtwide data analyses.

STEP 1: PREDICTING What are some predictions you have about how your students performed on this assessment? Why do you think so?	
STEP 2: VIEWING THE DATA Are there any patterns of achievement? What do you notice about the results over time? Do certain groups or individuals fare better or worse than others? Are there outliers? What trends or overall patterns do you notice?	
STEP 3: ANALYZING THE RESULTS Which students need additional time or support? Compare students or groups with variances in success. What contributed to the difference? Did the adults' approaches differ? What inferences can we make? What is an area where our team's students struggled? What contributed to these struggles?	
STEP 4: ACTION PLANNING What actions can we take immediately to provide support to students who need it now? What adaptations can we make for future teaching and learning events? What other steps can we take to improve the results of our work?	

From P. Hall, D. Childs-Bowen, A. Cunningham-Morris, P. Pajardo, & A. Simeral, *The Principal Influence: A Framework for Developing Leadership Capacity in Principals* (Alexandria, VA: ASCD, 2016). © 2016 ASCD.

APPENDIX B.7: MONEY TALKS RUNNING RECORD

DIRECTIONS: This tool enables principals to analyze expenses to determine their impact on SIP goals and articulate the school's specific needs. Utilize this Money Talks data to inform future decision making and guide budgetary allocations or reallocations of school and district budgets.

GUIDING QUESTIONS	Q1 OR 1ST 9 WEEKS	Q2 OR 2ND 9 WEEKS	Q3 OR 3RD 9 WEEKS	Q4 OR 4TH 9 WEEKS
What are my schools' needs for this quarter/9 weeks?				
What data do I have to support this identified need?				
What resources will be needed to address this need?				
What outcomes do I expect if resources were available for this need?				
How will I assess the impact of the resources if applied to this need?				

From P. Hall, D. Childs-Bowen, A. Cunningham-Morris, P. Pajardo, & A. Simeral, *The Principal Influence: A Framework for Developing Leadership Capacity in Principals* (Alexandria, VA: ASCD, 2016). © 2016 ASCD.

APPENDIX B.8: STAGES OF CONCERN

PURPOSE: The Stages of Concern tool consists of and describes seven categories of possible concerns related to an innovation. People who are in the earlier stages of a change process will likely have more self-focused concerns, such as worries about whether they can learn a new program or how it will affect their job performance. As individuals become more comfortable with and skilled in using an innovation, their concerns shift to focus on broader impacts, such as how the initiative will affect their students or their working relationships with colleagues.

DIRECTIONS: With the Stages of Concern tool as a guide, leaders engage stakeholders in reflective dialogue (one-on-one, in small groups, or at a staff meeting) about different elements of the innovation. As participants respond, leaders gather data that inform future support and implementation efforts. Leaders are also able to follow up with stakeholders by asking what they need to fully engage in the innovation.

STAGE OF CONCERN		TYPICAL STATEMENT
0: Unconcerned	Unrelated	"I think I heard something about it, but I'm too busy right now with other priorities to be concerned about it."
1: Informational	Self	"This seems interesting, and I would like to know more about it."
2: Personal	Self	"I'm concerned about the changes I'll need to make in my routines."
3: Management	Task	"I'm concerned about how much time it takes to get ready to teach with this new approach."
4: Consequence	Impact	"How will this new approach affect my students?"
5: Collaboration	Impact	"I'm looking forward to sharing some ideas about it with other teachers."
6: Refocusing	Impact	"I have some ideas about something that would work even more effectively."

From P. Hall, D. Childs-Bowen, A. Cunningham-Morris, P. Pajardo, & A. Simeral, *The Principal Influence: A Framework for Developing Leadership Capacity in Principals* (Alexandria, VA: ASCD, 2016). © 2016 ASCD. Used with permission from SEDL, an Affiliate of American Institutes for Research; original document available at http://www.sedl.org/cbam/stages_of_concern.html.

APPENDIX B.9: PROTOCOL FOR CLARIFYING DIP AND SIP ALIGNMENT

PURPOSE: Early in the cycle of SIP development, district supervisors convene principals during a regularly scheduled management or professional development session to increase clarity with the District Improvement Plan (DIP, or Strategic Plan) and SIPs for vertical and horizontal alignment. (*Note:* This protocol is *not* intended to create a new district school improvement plan, mission or vision statement.)

MATERIALS: Chart paper, markers (large and felt-tip), yarn, large and medium sticky notes of varying colors or sticky note cards of varying colors are also a possibility. Each principal should bring a copy of his or her draft SIP along with the DIP the principal has reviewed. Provide round table seating and comfortable chairs for teams of five to six principals at each. *Note:* Seating principals by feeder pattern schools or by grade band levels (elementary, middle, high) can yield strategic and collaboratively focused conversation.

STEP 1: As pre-reading material, provide each principal a copy of the District Improvement Plan (DIP), asking them to highlight big ideas and salient or important information to them.

STEP 2: During the session, post copies of the district mission and vision statements on chart paper for each table group. Each table group identifies a facilitator, recorder, and reporter. The facilitator asks all participants at the table to share (in round-robin format) the big ideas they highlighted. As a table group, agree on the top five big ideas that arose from the DIP. Then, as a whole group, each reporter shares his or her table group's main ideas. District supervisors listen for patterns and highlight them in the summary debrief.

STEP 3: Review participants' understanding of the purpose of a vision statement and a mission statement. Ask each group to write each of their top five big ideas on separate sticky notes (two sets), and place one on the vision statement chart and the other on the mission statement chart. Using yarn or markers, connect the identified big ideas to the vision and mission, possibly identifying any gaps or mismatches. Group thoughts or comments can be recorded directly on the chart.

STEP 4: Allow time for all participants to proceed around the room for a gallery walk, gathering additional ideas or uncovered gaps from the other groups. As teams return to their tables, allow time for them to discuss individual observations. Supervisors can allow time for a whole-group debrief summarizing the collective observations regarding alignment.

Continued

APPENDIX B.9: PROTOCOL FOR CLARIFYING DIP AND SIP ALIGNMENT (CONTINUED)

STEP 5:   The process is repeated; however, now the principals take their SIPs and capture the big ideas or intentions (each on a separate sticky note; it is helpful visually if each principal has a different color of sticky notes). When completed, each principal shares with the table group, posting his or her sticky notes under the DIP big ideas on the larger chart. At the completion, the facilitator opens up a table dialogue about observations (connectivity, alignment, mismatches, and/or gaps).

STEP 6:   Lead another gallery walk so principals can gauge the group's collective alignment. When principals return to their table groups, provide prompts to initiate dialogue around observations, connectivity, and horizontal alignment noticed across groups. Supervisors can then provide an opportunity for reporters from each group to share a summary of the table conversations. As a final reflection, supervisors can provide some quiet reflective writing time for each principal to reflect on and record how well his or her SIP aligns to the school's mission and vision.

From P. Hall, D. Childs-Bowen, A. Cunningham-Morris, P. Pajardo, & A. Simeral, *The Principal Influence: A Framework for Developing Leadership Capacity in Principals* (Alexandria, VA: ASCD, 2016). © 2016 ASCD.

APPENDIX B.10: TUNING PROTOCOL

PURPOSE:

The Tuning Protocol features time for the presenter to talk while participants are silent, and time for the participants to talk while the presenter is silent. It provides three levels of depth: presentation, participant discussion, and presenter reflection, and it is finalized by a general debriefing that can extend the conversation. This protocol can range anywhere from 30 minutes to 2 hours (typically it lasts about 1 hour).

STEP 1:

Introduction (first time only, 5 minutes)

- If participants don't usually work together, they briefly introduce themselves.
- Facilitator briefly introduces information about and guidelines for protocols, and establishes time limits for steps.

STEP 2:

Presentation (15 minutes)

- Presenter sets the context, describing the teaching/learning situation, while participants take notes.
- Presenter shares materials related to the teaching/learning situation described, including student work. The presenter should use part of the presentation time to let participants examine what is being presented.
- Presenter poses one or two key questions about the teaching/learning situation.

STEP 3:

Clarifying Questions (5 minutes)

- Participants ask nonevaluative questions about the presentation (e.g., "What happened before X? What did you do next? What did Y say?").
- Facilitator guards against questions that approach evaluation (e.g., "Why didn't you try X?"). Participants who ask evaluative questions may be invited to rephrase the questions as clarifying or to save the questions for the participant discussion step.
- It is entirely possible that the group will not get all its questions answered—there is never enough time!—but participants will have enough information at this stage for the protocol to be productive.

STEP 4:

Individual Writing (5 minutes)

Both the presenter and the participants write about the presentation, addressing the key question(s). This step helps each participant focus and have something to say during the participant discussion.

Continued

APPENDIX B.10: TUNING PROTOCOL (CONTINUED)

STEP 5:

Participant Discussion (15 minutes)

- Participants discuss issues raised during the presentation among themselves, striving to deepen their understanding of the situation and seeking answers to the question(s) posed by the presenter.
- The presenter is silent, taking notes on what the participants say.
- Participants should strive for a balance of warm and cool feedback unless instructed differently by the presenter.
- Participants should strive for substantive discourse. They should not engage in a round-robin discussion, but rather focus on and develop one idea at a time.
- The facilitator should keep an eye on the individual airtime of participants and ensure that their focus is on the work being discussed rather than on the presenter.
- Participants "own" the situation discussed during this step; it is theirs to improve, with the presenter listening in silently and taking notes.

STEP 6:

Presenter Reflection (10 minutes)

- The presenter reflects aloud on the participants' discussion, using the issues the participants raised to deepen understanding and reflecting on possible answers to questions posed. The presenter can also suggest future actions, questions, dilemmas, and so forth, and may correct any misunderstandings.
- Participants silently take notes on the presenter reflection.

STEP 7:

Debriefing (5 minutes)

- The presenter discusses how well the protocol worked and thanks the participants for their support.
- Participants discuss how well they think the protocol worked and thank the presenter for bringing the work to them to be tuned.
- The presenter and participants engage in more general discussion of both the situation examined and the protocol process itself.

From P. Hall, D. Childs-Bowen, A. Cunningham-Morris, P. Pajardo, & A. Simeral, *The Principal Influence: A Framework for Developing Leadership Capacity in Principals* (Alexandria, VA: ASCD, 2016). © 2016 ASCD. Original source: L. Easton, *Protocols for professional learning* (Alexandria, VA: ASCD, 2009).

APPENDIX B.11: CONTINUOUS IMPROVEMENT CYCLE

PURPOSE:
The Plan-Do-Study-Act (PDSA) cycle is intended to provide information (data) about a change and assess the impact of its implementation. Schools and districts can use this to monitor short-term and long-term school improvement plans, instructional cycles, and other innovations. Individual teachers and teams can also use this tool to guide unit development, instructional techniques, individualized learning plans, and other innovations.

DIRECTIONS:
Follow the simple four steps of the PDSA cycle as often as necessary to gauge the effects of a plan, innovation, or change.

STEP 1: PLAN
With a clearly determined outcome in mind, create a thorough plan to accomplish this goal. To help with this step, consider the creation of a SMART goal: strategic, measurable, attainable (or aggressive), results-oriented, and time-bound. Guiding questions might include the following: What are we trying to accomplish? How will we measure our success? How will we attempt to meet this goal? When will we check our progress?

STEP 2: DO
Following the strategies outlined in the plan, implement the action steps. Fidelity to the plan is important, as it provides consistent and reliable feedback for the following steps in the cycle. A suggested timeline for collecting data might include 3-week, 6-week, and 9-week intervals (these can be modified of course).

STEP 3: STUDY
As the plan unfolds, it is important to collect evidence and analyze the impact of the innovation, change, or plan. Use the measurable data source from the SMART goal to guide this step. Guiding questions might include these: What changes in outcomes have we seen since implementing this plan? Do these changes reflect an improvement? How so? Which elements of the plan are more impactful than others? What are some potential modifications that might increase the positive effect of this plan?

STEP 4: ACT
Using the evidence from Step 3 of the PDSA cycle, take action to (a) refine the plan, (b) abandon the plan, (c) continue the plan in order to collect more data, or (d) prepare for full implementation (as necessary).

(Repeat the PDSA cycle as necessary.)

Continued

APPENDIX B.11: CONTINUOUS IMPROVEMENT CYCLE (CONTINUED)

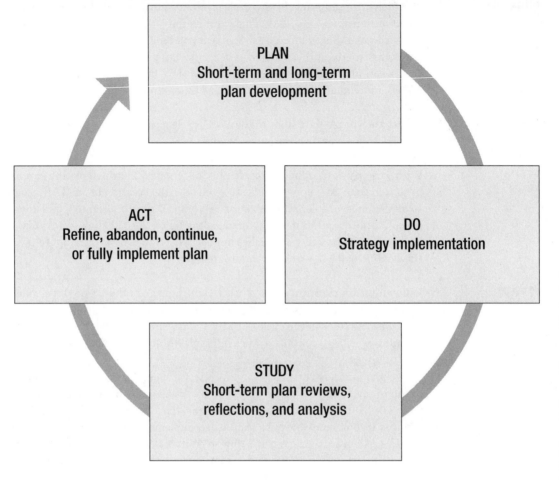

From P. Hall, D. Childs-Bowen, A. Cunningham-Morris, P. Pajardo, & A. Simeral, *The Principal Influence: A Framework for Developing Leadership Capacity in Principals* (Alexandria, VA: ASCD, 2016). © 2016 ASCD. Original source: L. Easton, *Protocols for professional learning* (Alexandria, VA: ASCD, 2009).

APPENDIX B.12: TIPS FOR CONSENSUS BUILDING

PURPOSE:
Establishing consensus is critical when the commitment of the group is essential to the success of a plan, approach, or prioritized actions. A first step for leaders is to facilitate the agreed-upon definition of "consensus" among all the participants. Once that is clear, the process for achieving consensus should be agreed upon by all stakeholders as well. This tool provides tips and steps for building consensus within a group of any size.

DIRECTIONS:

STEP 1:
Define consensus.
Each participant writes his or her definition of the term "consensus," and then partners with another individual to refine and rewrite their common definition. Each pair then partners with another pair, combining and refining their definitions into a new blended definition for the foursome. This process repeats until the entire group reaches a single definition of the term.

STEP 2:
Brainstorming discussion.
Allow time to discuss the issue at hand, letting all participants provide perspectives, data, research, and/or opinions. Make sure all members have equal opportunity to share and contribute to the discussion.

STEP 3:
Synthesize main points.
Look for similarities in thinking, building upon, one another's ideas and adapting to include different points of view. Using a public display of summary points (e.g., on chart paper) helps participants see that perspectives are honored.

STEP 4:
Recommend action.
Work toward recommendations or decisions that are accepted by all members of the group. Where disagreements exist, engage the entire group in moving to a win-win solution.

STEP 5:
Collect evidence of support.
In order to make sure each group member can live with the recommendation or decisions, it is important that each individual respond. The leader/facilitator should ask a question such as the following: Do you support this decision, or can you live with it and support it? Strategies that can be used include:
- » Verbally: indicating in a round-robin fashion how they support the decision
- » Nonverbally: Using a "fist-to-five" method (zero fingers indicates refusal to support, five fingers indicates full endorsement, and a 0–5 scale in between)

Continued

APPENDIX B.12: TIPS FOR CONSENSUS BUILDING (CONTINUED)

NOTE:	Consensus building has no voting and no power plays—not even by the leader. The entire process is transparent and open, illustrating the group's willingness to receive all perspectives and act in the entire group's best interests.
RESPONDING TO "NO"	When and if someone responds that he or she is unable or unwilling to support the proposed decision, the leader/facilitator should ask what would it take (what adaptations are needed) to enable that person to support the decision? At this point, the process moves back to step 3 where the group collectively makes adaptations as needed. The group may ask the dissenting opinion holder to support the decision as best as possible (without blocking or obstructing the process) for a trial period, after which the group checks back in. The group often commits to helping the individual to move to support the consensus decision through this type of support.

From P. Hall, D. Childs-Bowen, A. Cunningham-Morris, P. Pajardo, & A. Simeral, *The Principal Influence: A Framework for Developing Leadership Capacity in Principals* (Alexandria, VA: ASCD, 2016). © 2016 ASCD.

APPENDIX B.13: FUNNELING CONSENSUS MODEL

PURPOSE: The Funneling Consensus Model is a means of building consensus through an iterative series of questionnaires on a specific topic that lead to consensus. Consider this tool a way to "funnel" many ideas into the most pressing, useful, or important ideas. This will lead to a decision that incorporates all perspectives and is ultimately based on the most vital information.

DIRECTIONS:

ROUND 1:   Formulate either an open-ended question or structured question that addresses the core of the topic at hand. For instance: "What are the most important factors for educators to consider in preparing students for constructed-response assessments?" All participants contribute to the brainstorming process, accessing extensive research, a review of the literature, published expert opinions, personal experiences, and their own expertise. This is an open-ended brainstorming process meant to surface all possible solutions and/or ideas. Post participant responses on chart paper or in another easily viewed format.

ROUND 2:   Synthesizing the vast contributions from Round 1, create a prioritized list of topics, factors, or questions. Ask participants to rank-order the items in terms of importance for their school, grade level, or department area. For example, continuing with the theme of the original question in Round 1, listings might include (a) "Students are able to discern easily and quickly the core question in the prompt," (b) "Students are able to add detail, using evidence from the text to support their response," and (c) "Students are able to draw a conclusion or summarize the contents of the response in relationship to the core question." If some of the original brainstormed suggestions are related, link them together to avoid duplication.

NOTE: Round 2 can be repeated as many times as necessary to "funnel" the original brainstorm into a more manageable list.

ROUND 3:   The final list, based on rankings from Round 2, is distributed for consensus confirmation. Any last-minute advocacy or dissenting opinions (substantiated by data or research) may be considered by the principal or team before moving to action on the topic.

From P. Hall, D. Childs-Bowen, A. Cunningham-Morris, P. Pajardo, & A. Simeral, *The Principal Influence: A Framework for Developing Leadership Capacity in Principals* (Alexandria, VA: ASCD, 2016). © 2016 ASCD.

APPENDIX B.14: NAVIGATING DIFFICULT SITUATIONS

PURPOSE: Every meeting, and every team, has the potential for the emergence of a difficult situation. This table is intended to provide guidance to leaders/facilitators as they work to conduct their business as seamlessly and productively as possible. To limit the interruptions from difficult meeting participants, start by arranging a private, one-on-one conversation. The following table should guide how leaders/facilitators handle certain scenarios:

TYPES OF MEETING PARTICIPANTS	METHODS OF PRODUCTIVELY HANDLING THIS TYPE OF PARTICIPANT
THE NAYSAYER (Someone who reflexively disagrees with the suggestions of others)	√ Ask the naysayer what alternatives he or she would propose. √ Ask the group for opinions on the naysayer's comments. √ Ask the naysayer, "What would have to change for the proposed solution to work?" (Do not accept "It won't work" as a response.)
THE AGGRESSOR (Someone who expresses disagreement inappropriately)	√ Remind the aggressor to limit comments to ideas rather than people. √ Refer the aggressor to the staff's agreed-upon norms of behavior for meetings. √ Ask other participants if they agree with the aggressor's statements. √ If the aggressor's comment is not directed at an individual, ignore it until the break, when you can speak privately. √ If the statement is made directly to you, be professional and respectful. Acknowledge that there are different ways to think about any given topic. Avoid becoming defensive or getting drawn into an argument.
THE DOMINATOR (Someone who dominates discussions with redundant or unnecessarily long responses)	√ Break eye contact with the dominator and call on someone else by name to provide a suggestion. √ Impose a time limit on all staff members' responses. √ When the dominator pauses for breath, take the opportunity to ask for someone else's opinion. √ Hold your hand up, palm facing outward. √ Post a flip chart on the wall at the beginning of every meeting and label it "Parking Lot." Put sticky notes in easily accessible locations. When a participant exhibits the characteristics of a dominator, write down his or her comment on the sticky note and place it on the flip chart. At the end of the meeting, review the comments with the dominator.
THE ATTENTION SEEKER (Someone who feels the need to be the focal point at meetings)	√ Ask attention seekers to help with tasks such as demonstrations, thus using their desire for attention to your advantage. √ If the attention-seeking behavior is not disruptive, ignore it (e.g., by turning your back to the attention seeker).

THE AVOIDER (Someone who cannot or will not focus at meetings)	√ Start meetings on time and with engaging activities. √ Have staff members catch up with you after the meeting or during breaks if they need to be informed of what they've missed. √ Arrange the physical environment so that you can make eye contact with all staff members at all times. √ When avoiders engage in side conversations, walk toward them casually while continuing to lead the meeting; then stand near them until they cease talking. √ When a staff member appears reluctant to participate in a large-group activity, address him or her directly.

From P. Hall, D. Childs-Bowen, A. Cunningham-Morris, P. Pajardo, & A. Simeral, *The Principal Influence: A Framework for Developing Leadership Capacity in Principals* (Alexandria, VA: ASCD, 2016). © 2016 ASCD. Adapted from p. 28 of M. Jennings, *Leading effective meetings, teams, and work groups in districts and schools* (Alexandria, VA: ASCD, 2007).

APPENDIX B.15: DEVELOPING RESULTS-BASED PLCS

DIRECTIONS: Guide principals through the analysis of the level of implementation and impact of Professional Learning Communities (PLCs) within their school and district. Use the information collected to guide planning steps to further implement collaborative, results-oriented PLC leadership efforts.

Describe how Professional Learning Communities fit into current and established district priorities.	
How does the district measure the effectiveness of site-based PLCs?	
What data are collected by the district to provide evidence of effectiveness?	
How do you, as principal, measure the effectiveness of your site-based PLCs?	
What data do you collect to provide evidence of PLC effectiveness?	
What specific behaviors and/or practices are necessary for you to effectively support site-based PLCs?	
What specific district expectations are necessary to ensure that all principals are engaging in those behaviors and/or practices?	
All principals require differentiated support to meet district expectations. What specific support(s) do you need to increase your PLC leadership effectiveness?	
Who will provide that support to you?	
When, and how often, will that support be provided to you?	
What other factors are important to consider? What other information should we note?	

From P. Hall, D. Childs-Bowen, A. Cunningham-Morris, P. Pajardo, & A. Simeral, *The Principal Influence: A Framework for Developing Leadership Capacity in Principals* (Alexandria, VA: ASCD, 2016). © 2016 ASCD.

APPENDIX B.16: INDIVIDUAL PROFESSIONAL DEVELOPMENT PLANNING TEMPLATE

DIRECTIONS: This tool aids in the development of individual teachers' capacity-building efforts. Principals and teachers (and coaches, as applicable) complete the form together, creating a collaborative plan based on results and enhancing the teacher's growth as a reflective practitioner.

PART 1: REFLECTIVE STAGE	**Name of teacher**	**Stage on Continuum of Self-Reflection**	**What descriptors indicate the teacher reflects in that stage?**
		☐ Unaware ☐ Conscious ☐ Action ☐ Refinement	
PART 2: FOCUS AREA	**Focus area for goal setting**	**What data indicate this is an appropriate goal? (Consider data sources and current levels of performance/achievement.)**	
PART 3: TECHNICAL GOAL	**Write a SMART goal based on teacher performance and/or student achievement, based on Part 2 responses.**		
PART 4: REFLECTIVE GOAL	**What is the teacher's capacity-building goal for his/her stage on the Continuum of Self-Reflection?**		
	☐ If Unaware stage, the goal is to build deeper awareness of students, content, and pedagogy. ☐ If Conscious stage, the goal is to work with greater intentionality in addressing student needs, content, and pedagogy. ☐ If Action stage, the goal is to build on experience and help strengthen expertise through accurate assessment of instructional impact. ☐ If Refinement stage, the goal is to encourage long-term growth and continued reflection through responsiveness to ongoing assessments.		

Continued

APPENDIX B.16: INDIVIDUAL PROFESSIONAL DEVELOPMENT PLANNING TEMPLATE (CONTINUED)

PART 5: SELF-DIRECTED ACTION STEPS	What self-directed steps will the teacher tackle in order to meet these goals?		
PART 6: ADMINISTRATIVE SUPPORT	What support will the teacher's administrator (principal, assistant principal, etc.) provide?	How will this support be provided?	How often will this support be provided?
PART 7: COACHING/PEER SUPPORT	What support will the teacher's instructional coach (mentor, department chair, etc.) and/or peer teammates provide?	How will this support be provided?	How often will this support be provided?

APPENDIX B.17: DIFFERENTIATED FEEDBACK BY STAGE

PURPOSE: Use this document as a guide for selecting the language and feedback prompts that match the teacher's stage on the Continuum of Self-Reflection. By using the stems and prompts included here, leaders are able to launch conversations that generate reflective thought in teachers and match their needs as reflective practitioners.

UNAWARE STAGE

CAPACITY-BUILDING GOAL: TO BUILD DEEPER AWARENESS OF STUDENTS, CONTENT, AND PEDAGOGY

- ☐ When you did _____, the students did _____. It worked because _____. Do that again!
- ☐ I noticed you used _____ and it was effective because _____. use it whenever you want your students to _____.
- ☐ When you did _____, the students did _____. Tomorrow, try _____, and tell me what happens.
- ☐ Your lesson was successful today because _____.
- ☐ You (or your students) struggled today because _____. Next time that happens, try this: _____. Then tell me what happens.
- ☐ You appear frustrated with _____, and I noticed that you _____ several times. Tomorrow, try to take note of how many times you _____. Then let's chat further.
- ☐ I observed _____, which is not what you/we were going for in that lesson; try _____ to get the lesson back on track. This usually works because _____.

CONSCIOUS STAGE

CAPACITY-BUILDING GOAL: TO WORK WITH GREATER INTENTIONALITY IN ADDRESSING STUDENT NEEDS, CONTENT, AND PEDAGOGY

- ☐ Your goal is _____. How can I help you keep that focus and support your efforts?
- ☐ I see you were using _____ today. Keep that focus! What worked well today?
- ☐ Tell me about the purpose of today's activity. What is your evidence of success?
- ☐ Today, your students were successful at _____. What did you do that directly led to their success?
- ☐ I noticed _____ today. How might the outcomes change if you tried _____? Give it a shot and let me know how it goes.
- ☐ Yesterday I observed your students _____; today, they are _____. How do you determine your daily lesson structure?
- ☐ Tell me more about the planning that went into today's lesson. Why did you select the strategy you chose for this lesson?
- ☐ How do you use what you know about your students to drive lesson planning each day?
- ☐ When you _____ today, I observed several students _____. How will you shift tomorrow's lesson to change the outcomes?
- ☐ How does this lesson connect to prior and future student learning objectives?
- ☐ What misconceptions might students have during tomorrow's lesson? How will you address that in your planning?

Continued

APPENDIX B.17: DIFFERENTIATED FEEDBACK BY STAGE
(CONTINUED)

ACTION STAGE

CAPACITY-BUILDING GOAL: TO BUILD ON EXPERIENCE AND HELP STRENGTHEN EXPERTISE THROUGH ACCURATE ASSESSMENT OF INSTRUCTIONAL IMPACT

- ☐ What was the purpose of today's activity? Was it successful? How do you know?
- ☐ Which parts of today's lesson went well? Which parts didn't? Why?
- ☐ What was the goal of today's lesson? How did you determine that goal?
- ☐ Today, I observed you _____. Did that contribute to your goal? How can you tell?
- ☐ Why did you choose to _____ today? Was that strategy effective? How do you know?
- ☐ What other strategy could you have used today to achieve your goals?
- ☐ How do you predetermine what your evidence of success will be for a lesson?
- ☐ Do your anecdotal observations of student learning align with more formal assessment data?
- ☐ If you could teach this lesson again, what would you do differently? Why?
- ☐ Which students successfully achieved today's learning target? Which students struggled? Why was that so?
- ☐ What does the student work from today's lesson tell you about _____ as a learner?
- ☐ What can you tell me about _____ as a learner? How can you find out more?

REFINEMENT STAGE

CAPACITY-BUILDING GOAL: TO ENCOURAGE LONG-TERM GROWTH AND CONTINUED REFLECTION THROUGH RESPONSIVENESS TO ONGOING ASSESSMENTS

- ☐ Today, your students _____, and you immediately responded with _____. How did you plan to address that misconception?
- ☐ In the middle of today's lesson, you abruptly changed course. What led to that decision? Was it a successful move? How do you know?
- ☐ How do you know when students are learning in the middle of a lesson? What do you look for?
- ☐ How do you identify specific learning styles of the students in your room?
- ☐ Explain the thinking that went into planning a lesson such as this. How do you know which strategies to select? How do you decide on which activities to choose?
- ☐ To what extent are you collaborating with your colleagues to plan and deliver your lessons? How can you become more intentional in partnering with your teammates?
- ☐ Your lesson today reminded me of a recent article I read in *Educational Leadership*. I'll put a copy in your box. I would love to hear your thoughts.

From P. Hall, D. Childs-Bowen, A. Cunningham-Morris, P. Pajardo, & A. Simeral, *The Principal Influence: A Framework for Developing Leadership Capacity in Principals* (Alexandria, VA: ASCD, 2016). © 2016 ASCD. Adapted and reprinted from p. 148 of P. Hall, & A. Simeral, *Building Teachers' Capacity for Success: A Collaborative Approach for Coaches and School Leaders* (Alexandria, VA: ASCD, 2008).

APPENDIX B.18: CONSULTANCY PROTOCOL

PURPOSE: One purpose of this protocol is to learn how others understand a dilemma and frame responses to it. The protocol may help the presenter address the dilemma or solve a problem, and the discourse may sound like asking for and getting advice, but the primary purpose of the Consultancy Protocol is to open up people's minds to new ways of thinking about problems and issues related to teaching and learning.

NUMBER OF PARTICIPANTS: A single group of 8–10 participants plus the presenter and facilitator is ideal.

TIME REQUIRED: Part 1 (individual writing) time varies. The time required for the Part 2 discussion is 45–60 minutes.

Part 1—Writing About the Dilemma:

This portion is completed individually before coming to the protocol group.

STEP 1: Considering the Dilemma. It should be an issue with which people are struggling, that has a way to go before being resolved, that is up to them to control, and that it is critical to their work.

STEP 2: Writing About the Dilemma. The National School Reform Faculty (NSRF) offers these questions to guide the writing ("Consultancy Protocol," n.d., ¶ 4):

— Why is this a dilemma for you? Why is this dilemma important to you?

— If you could take a snapshot of this dilemma, what would you/we see?

— What have you done already to try to remedy the dilemma, and what are the results of those attempts?

— Who do you hope changes? Who do you hope will take action to resolve this dilemma? You will want to present a dilemma that is about your practice, actions, behaviors, beliefs, and assumptions, and not someone else's.

— What do you assume to be true about this dilemma, and how have these assumptions influenced your thinking about the dilemma?

STEP 3: Stating the Dilemma as a Focusing Question That Gets to the Heart of the Matter. Here is an example offered by the NSRF: Dilemma: Teachers love doing projects with students, but the projects never seem to connect to one another or have very coherent educational goals; they are just fun. Question: How do I work with teachers so they move to deep learning about important concepts while still staying connected to hands-on learning?

Continued

APPENDIX B.18: CONSULTANCY PROTOCOL (CONTINUED)

Part 2—The Consultancy Process
(suggested times based on a 50-minute session)

STEP 1: **Presenter Overview** (10 minutes)

- The presenter gives an overview of the dilemma along with a focus question for the group to consider.
- The presenter may provide participants with a paper one page or shorter in length describing the dilemma.

STEP 2: **Clarifying Questions** (5 minutes)

- Participants ask clarifying questions of the presenter—questions that can be answered with facts.

STEP 3: **Probing Questions** (5 minutes)

- The group asks probing questions that help the presenter expand thinking about the dilemma.
- The presenter does not have to respond to the questions. If the presenter does respond, the participants do not discuss the answers.

STEP 4: **Participant Discussion** (15 minutes)

- The presenter withdraws from the group, taking notes on the participants' discussion.
- Participants might describe possible actions that the presenter might take, but they should not decide on a solution. Their job is simply to refine the issues for the presenter.
- The NSRF suggests the following questions to get the discussion going ("Consultancy Protocol," n.d., ¶ 7):
  — What did we hear?
  — What didn't we hear that we think might be relevant?
  — What assumptions seem to be operating?
  — What questions does the dilemma raise for us?
  — What do we think about the dilemma?
  — What might we do or try if faced with a similar dilemma? What have we done in similar situations?

STEP 5: **Presenter Reflection** (10 minutes)

- Referring to notes taken during the participant discussion, the presenter reflects on what the participants said and how their comments have affected his or her thinking.
- It is particularly important for the presenter to share new insights that the discussion has provided. The presenter might even discover that the question offered at the end of the presentation has changed!

STEP 6: **Debriefing** (5 minutes).
The facilitator leads the group in discussion of the protocol process and invites the presenter and participants to continue refining the dilemma.

From P. Hall, D. Childs-Bowen, A. Cunningham-Morris, P. Pajardo, & A. Simeral, *The Principal Influence: A Framework for Developing Leadership Capacity in Principals* (Alexandria, VA: ASCD, 2016). © 2016 ASCD. Adapted and reprinted from p. 50 of L. Easton, (2009). *Protocols for Professional Learning* (Alexandria, VA: ASCD, 2009).

APPENDIX B.19: DOT PROTOCOL

PURPOSE: The Dot Protocol is designed to help groups arrive at consensus or a common understanding. For example, this protocol could be used to help identify priorities in a School Improvement Plan or to achieve an agreed-upon definition of a "best practice" in instruction.

PROCESS:

STEP 1: **Investigate the research.**
After identifying the topic at hand, compile book excerpts, articles, videos, and other resources that highlight the research and information about the topic. As a staff, or within grade-level or content teams, engage in collaborative inquiry (reading together, addressing questions that arise through the review of the research).

STEP 2: **Blend experience and expertise into the discussion.**
Bring the staff together to share their own experience and/or expertise with the topic at hand. As appropriate, staff can share by writing on chart paper their responses to any or all of the following prompts, based on a combination of their own personal experiences, professional expertise, and the review of the research completed in Step 1:

1. What does the topic look like in practice?
2. What does the topic sound like in practice?
3. What is the outcome of this topic when implemented successfully?

STEP 3: **Prioritize the elements.**
Distribute three sticky-dots (the kind you can pick up at an office supply store) to each participant. Instruct them to place their sticky-dots next to the written responses that have the greatest likelihood to achieve success. Participants can "vote" for three different responses, or they can combine their votes for one or two extra-powerful written responses.

STEP 4: **Compile the highest-leverage list.**
Together, as a staff or grade-level or content team, identify the five to six elements that received the most votes (it could be more or less than that, depending on how the sticky-dot voting turned out). Rewrite them on a new piece of chart paper to post for the staff.

STEP 5: **Set the expectation.**
The revised list becomes the consensus or common understanding for the staff. As the leader, establish the expectation that this list has authentic power—it is the will of the group—and should trump any other individual element. For example, if the Dot Protocol is used to clarify a best practice in instruction, the final list would become the standard for exemplary performance and would be expected when the strategy is implemented. This would also become a focus for additional professional development, coaching, and strategic feedback.

From P. Hall, D. Childs-Bowen, A. Cunningham-Morris, P. Pajardo, & A. Simeral, *The Principal Influence: A Framework for Developing Leadership Capacity in Principals* (Alexandria, VA: ASCD, 2016). © 2016 ASCD.

APPENDIX B.20: GUIDELINES FOR INSTRUCTIONAL ROUNDS

PURPOSE:

Instructional Rounds is a strategy used to foster collaboration and to build teachers' collective capacity. By engaging in this practice, teachers expand their repertoire of skills, gain a greater appreciation for their colleagues' instructional practices, and engage in reflective dialogue about teaching approaches.

PART I:

Conducting Rounds

Groups conducting rounds are usually small in numbers—three to five, not counting the lead teachers. On the day on which rounds are scheduled, teachers being observed alert their classes that they will have some other teachers visiting their classroom. Observed teachers might explain to their students that teachers in the building are trying to learn from one another just as students learn from one another.

When the observer teachers enter a classroom, they knock at the door and quietly move to some portion of the classroom that does not disrupt the flow of instruction. This is usually somewhere at the back of the classroom. There they observe what is occurring and make notes on their observational forms.

At the end of the observation, the observer team exits the classroom, making sure to thank the observed teacher and the students.

PART II:

Debriefing Rounds

After rounds have been conducted, members of the observing team convene to debrief on their experiences. They do so by discussing each observation, one at a time. This can be done in a round-robin format, where each observer teacher comments on what he or she noted. The leader of the rounds facilitates this process.

The leader starts by reminding everyone that the purpose of the discussion is not to evaluate the observed teacher. Rules regarding how to share observations should be established prior to the debriefing. Useful rules include:

- Comments made during the debriefing should not be shared with anyone.
- Do not offer suggestions to the observed teachers unless they explicitly ask for feedback.
- Nothing observed within a lesson should be shared with anyone.
- Observed teachers should be thanked and acknowledged for their willingness to open their classrooms to others.

As observer teachers take turns commenting on what they saw in a particular classroom, it is useful to use a "plus-delta" format. The observer teacher begins by noting the positive things (pluses) he or she observed in the classroom. Next, the observer can mention some questions (deltas) he or she had about the teacher's use of strategies. Finally, the observer compares and contrasts his or her classroom strategies with one or more of the techniques observed.

+	Δ

The process is completed for each classroom observed. For any particular observation, an observer teacher can opt not to share his or her analysis with the group. The debriefing should end with all observer teachers identifying one thing they might do differently in their classroom as a result of the rounds.

APPENDIX B.21: SCHOOL VISITATION OBSERVATION TEMPLATE

PURPOSE: This tool can be used when visitors observe in classrooms at a host school. The observations foster dialogue that enriches both the host and the visitors.

Observer name:_____ Observed school:_____

Date:_____ Purpose for visitation:_____

PART 1: **Collect observation data**

Instructional Strategy or Teacher Action observed (input):		Direct result of Teacher Action (output):	
Anecdotal notes:		Additional information from host school/ observed teacher:	

Instructional Strategy or Teacher Action observed (input):		Direct result of Teacher Action (output):	
Anecdotal notes:		Additional information from host school/ observed teacher:	

Instructional Strategy or Teacher Action observed (input):		Direct result of Teacher Action (output):	
Anecdotal notes:		Additional information from host school/ observed teacher:	

PART 2: **Debrief**

Within your observation team, discuss your observations. What key strategies, actions, and/or structures did you observe? How did they impact student behavior and/or learning? What implications are there for your school? What questions do you have for the observation team?

As part of the debrief, schedule some follow-up time with the host school principal, facilitator, and/or a team of staff. Ask any questions you may have about the creation or implementation of the strategies and structures you observed. Be sure to thank the host school for it's time and openness.

APPENDIX B.22: DATA ACTION MODEL OVERVIEW

PURPOSE: This Data Action Model demonstrates the schedule of data meetings that analyze the impact of particular instructional practices, curriculum structures, and/or intervention plans. This model can be effectively followed for courses (over the span of a semester or year), units (over the span of a few days to several months), or specific Student Learning Objectives (over a shorter span of up to a few days).

DIRECTIONS: As a team, follow the steps outlined under each Data Meeting (DM) heading. Repeat as necessary.

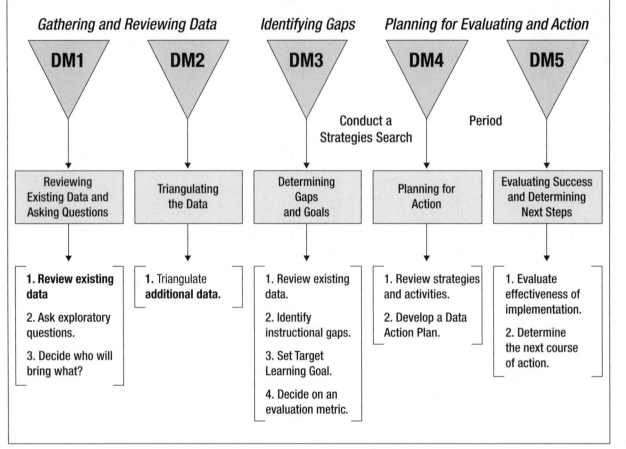

From P. Hall, D. Childs-Bowen, A. Cunningham-Morris, P. Pajardo, & A. Simeral, *The Principal Influence: A Framework for Developing Leadership Capacity in Principals* (Alexandria, VA: ASCD, 2016). © 2016 ASCD. Adapted and reprinted from p. 4 of D. Venables, *How Teachers Can Turn Data into Action* (Alexandria, VA: ASCD, 2014).

APPENDIX B.23: WHOLE CHILD PARTNERS INVENTORY

DIRECTIONS: As a leadership team, work together to create a list of school/community partnerships that might support the Whole Child approach. Brainstorm and discuss how each potential partner could provide support. Following the brainstorming and discussion, assign team members to reach out to those you have identified to invite them to an initial meeting to learn more about the Whole Child and how it could benefit students and families.

	HEALTHY	SAFE	ENGAGED	SUPPORTED	CHALLENGED
Community Colleges/ Universities					
Health and Human Services					
Business/ Corporate					
Service Learning Organizations					
Multi-Age Services Organizations					
Cultural Organizations					
Religious-Affiliated Organizations					
Others					

APPENDIX B.24: WHOLE CHILD PROBLEM-SOLVING AND DECISION-MAKING QUESTIONS

PURPOSE: These questions can be used to do a deep dive investigation into problems and decisions that may need to be addressed to achieve your Whole Child goals and annual performance targets.

DIRECTIONS: Assign sets of questions to small inquiry teams of leadership team members for their investigation and discussion. Have each inquiry team share their findings and conclusions at a district or school leadership team meeting. Use the inquiry team findings to determine areas that need to be addressed and next steps that must be taken in those areas in order to reach the district or school Whole Child goals.

1. What barriers and issues do we need to address to help each student enter school healthy?

2. How can we improve collaboration with schools in our feeder pattern to better help each student enter school healthy?

3. What are the barriers and issues we face in terms of making our school a healthy one?

4. What impedes families in our community from accessing needed health and human services? What decisions will we need to make to address these problems?

5. What problems are evident currently among individual students, subgroups of students, and our aggregate student body in terms of their choices about healthy behavior?

6. To what extent are health, nutrition, and physical fitness issues evident among our students?

7. To what extent are health, nutrition, and physical fitness issues evident among our staff members?

8. What problems exist in our staff members' understanding of how to model healthy choices and healthy lifestyles for our students?

9. What problems and impediments keep each of our students from experiencing their education as intellectually challenging?

10. How can we refine our ability to promote intellectual challenge for each of our students?

11. What problems exist in our school or district that detract from our learning environment being physically safe for all participants?

12. What problems exist in our school or district that detract from our learning environment being emotionally safe for all participants?

13. What barriers and issues keep each of our students from feeling engaged in their learning process?

14. What keeps students in our school or district from feeling connected to our school(s) and the learning environments they provide?

APPENDIX B.24: WHOLE CHILD PROBLEM-SOLVING AND DECISION-MAKING QUESTIONS (CONTINUED)

15. What issues and problems exist with our recruiting process for hiring new teachers?

16. What issues and problems exist with ensuring that each of our students works with qualified, caring adults?

17. What decisions are needed to improve our long-term professional development for our staff to ensure that each student works with qualified, caring adults?

18. What feedback do we get from employers in our community about the quality of our graduates who work for them?

19. How can we address identified problems and deficiencies in this area?

20. How successful are our students when they participate in postsecondary education (e.g., college, university, vocational school, military training)? What problems and gaps do we need to address in this area?

21. To what extent do our students graduate with competency in 21st century workplace skills and proficiencies? How do we know? What do we need to do to improve our understanding in this area?

From P. Hall, D. Childs-Bowen, A. Cunningham-Morris, P. Pajardo, & A. Simeral, *The Principal Influence: A Framework for Developing Leadership Capacity in Principals* (Alexandria, VA: ASCD, 2016). © 2016 ASCD. Adapted and reprinted from p. 46 of J. Brown, *Educating the Whole Child* (Alexandria, VA: ASCD, 2008).

APPENDIX B.25: CREATING A STRATEGIC COMMUNICATION PLAN

DIRECTIONS: Discuss the following communication goals, strategies, and vehicles. Add and modify as necessary, creating a plan to communicate openly, frequently, and effectively with key stakeholders and constituents.

GOAL 1:   Provide information about school programs, events, and activities.
Audience: Parents and families

STRATEGY	VEHICLES
Provide welcome message for new families and all families at the beginning of the school year	Welcome letter, email that can be personalized
Publish weekly newsletters with meeting notices, class news, menus, parenting tips	School website, social media channels (Facebook, Instagram, Twitter)
Prepare web page for the school with information about staff member's credentials, contact information, and program descriptions	School website
Others:	

GOAL 2:   Provide information about student progress, student learning, and achievement.
Audience: Parents and families

STRATEGY	VEHICLES
Prepare and send report cards and interim progress reports aligned with learning objectives and performance standards	Report cards; progress reports
Provide faculty with pads of notepaper for special handwritten notes to parents and families	Specially designed notepads
Prepare school profile data, distribute newsletters via email to opinion leaders and groups, and send reports to superintendent and board	
Provide unit plans and course syllabi to parents, emphasizing content standards and instruction planned for meeting standards	
Provide opportunities for faculty to learn effective conferencing techniques	
Others	

APPENDIX B.25: CREATING A STRATEGIC COMMUNICATION PLAN (CONTINUED)

GOAL 3: Provide information about helping children learn and succeed in school.
Audience: Parents, families, and community organizations

STRATEGY	VEHICLES
Include parenting tips, such as help with homework, recommended books, safety and health topics, and educational activities	Newsletter, website, community meetings, and social media channels (Facebook, Instagram, Twitter)
Inform parents and families about state standards, local curriculum and textbooks, student achievement testing, and school report cards	State Department of Education website, district website, school website, and newsletters
Invite parent participation in classroom activities, media center research activities, field trips, and special events	
Others:	

From P. Hall, D. Childs-Bowen, A. Cunningham-Morris, P. Pajardo, & A. Simeral, *The Principal Influence: A Framework for Developing Leadership Capacity in Principals* (Alexandria, VA: ASCD, 2016). © 2016 ASCD. Adapted and reprinted from p. 37 of A. Meek, R. Champion, & K. Dyer, *Guide for Instructional Leaders, Guide 3* (Alexandria, VA: ASCD, 2004).

APPENDIX B.26: CHANGE READINESS RUBRIC

DIRECTIONS: Gather information about each stakeholder group's perceptions, openness, and readiness to embrace a particular change initiative. Use this information to guide decision making, communication, and opportunities for additional learning.

DOMAIN	READY	INTERMEDIATE	NOT READY
HISTORY	Views previous changes as positive and generally successful.	Has no experience with previous change. Views previous change as having insignificant effect on group.	Views previous change as generally unsuccessful. Has negative experience.
NEED FOR CHANGE	Recognizes that present conditions are unacceptable and that change is required at this time if progress is to be made.	Realizes that things could be better but is not completely dissatisfied with things as they are.	Does not view present condition as so negative or troublesome that this change is required. May see need for others to change but not self.
WILLINGNESS TO CHANGE	Is willing to make difficult choices (personal and group) to bring about change will be difficult, possibly with a long period of discomfort.	Will change if the change does not require a significant inconvenience to group.	Sees no need to change. Is resistant to doing anything significantly different that may create discomfort for group.
FAITH IN LEADERSHIP	Believes that the current leaders have the ability to accomplish the change.	Has no strong opinions toward leadership either positive or negative due to past experience or lack of knowledge.	Is negative toward current leaders' capabilities and/or motives in general. Doesn't believe leaders can accomplish the change.

APPENDIX B.26: CHANGE READINESS RUBRIC (CONTINUED)

CHANGE PLAN	Has a good understanding of the vision for the future associated with the change plan. Believes that the change plan, as presented, has the potential to achieve the goal(s).	Does not have a clear understanding of the vision for the future associated with the change plan. Has doubts about major components of the change plan as the right approach to achieve the goal(s).	Does not agree with the vision of the future after the change. Does not believe the change plan, as presented, is necessary or has the potential to achieve the goal(s).
SKILLS NECESSARY TO IMPLEMENT	Believes the group represented has the knowledge and/or skills necessary to implement the plan.	Believes the group has some of the knowledge and/or skills necessary to implement the plan and believes that many of those who do not will be able to acquire the knowledge and/or skills.	Has serious doubts that the group represented has the knowledge and/or skills necessary to successfully implement the plan and doubts that most members of the group can acquire the knowledge and/or skills.

From P. Hall, D. Childs-Bowen, A. Cunningham-Morris, P. Pajardo, & A. Simeral, *The Principal Influence: A Framework for Developing Leadership Capacity in Principals* (Alexandria, VA: ASCD, 2016). © 2016 ASCD. Adapted and reprinted from p. 160 of D. Reeves, *Leading Change in Your School* (Alexandria, VA: ASCD, 2009).

APPENDIX B.27: FEARS AND HOPES: A CHANGE READINESS PERSPECTIVE

DIRECTIONS: Using this protocol early in any innovation with team members helps prepare them for expected outcomes to be celebrated and potential pitfalls and barriers to avoid or be cognizant of during implementation.

STEP 1: **Confront Fears**

a. Generate individually a list of your worries, concerns, or fears and write them on one side of an index card (or in this form) related to the innovation, issue, strategy, SIP, etc.

b. Use a round-robin format, with each person sharing one item at a time, to share your list with one another.

c. Validate participants' concerns without responding or attempting to address them right away.

d. Identify patterns that emerged.

STEP 2: **Embrace Hopes**

a. Generate individually a list of your hopes, dreams, and goals and write them on the opposite side of your index card (or in this form) related to the innovation, issue, strategy, SIP, etc.

b. Use a round-robin format, with each person sharing one item at a time, to share lists with one another.

c. Validate participants' hopes without expressing overconfidence or doubt right away.

d. Identify patterns that emerged.

STEP 3: **Action Planning**

a. Include the patterns (and individual responses) of hopes and fears throughout the early planning stages of a change initiative.

b. Revisit periodically during the implementation phase, adapting course as necessary to address fears and to support hopes.

From P. Hall, D. Childs-Bowen, A. Cunningham-Morris, P. Pajardo, & A. Simeral, *The Principal Influence: A Framework for Developing Leadership Capacity in Principals* (Alexandria, VA: ASCD, 2016). © 2016 ASCD.

APPENDIX B.28: CHANGE THEORY HIGHLIGHTS

DIRECTIONS: Below are theory elements and insights from three noted authors to ground principals in transition and change management. Highlight and investigate key elements. Select two to three elements and help principals plan how to leverage collaborative learning teams and professional development to lead and manage positive change experiences.

BRIDGES From *Managing transitions: Making the Most of Change* (1991)	KOTTER From *Leading Change* (1996)	FULLAN From *The Six Secrets of Change: What the Best Leaders Do to Help Their Organization Survive and Thrive* (2008)
Identify who's losing what	Establish a sense of urgency	Love your employees
Accept the reality and importance of the subjective lesson	Create the guiding coalition	Connect peers with purpose
Don't be surprised at "overreaction"	Develop a vision and strategy	Capacity building prevails
Acknowledge the losses openly and sympathetically	Communicate the change vision	Learning is the work
Expect and accept signs of grieving	Empower employees for broad-based action	Transparency rules
Compensate for the losses	Generate short-term wins	Systems learn
Give people information, and do it again and again	Consolidate gains and produce more change	
Define what's over and what isn't	Anchor new approaches in the culture	
Mark the endings		
Treat the past with respect		
Let people take a piece of the old way with them		
Show how endings ensure continuity of what really matters		

From P. Hall, D. Childs-Bowen, A. Cunningham-Morris, P. Pajardo, & A. Simeral, *The Principal Influence: A Framework for Developing Leadership Capacity in Principals* (Alexandria, VA: ASCD, 2016). © 2016 ASCD.

APPENDIX B.29: CHANGE MANAGEMENT QUESTIONNAIRE

DIRECTIONS: These questions below are designed to be used with various stakeholder groups to begin the discussion regarding the group's attitudes in each domain. The responses can be used with the Change Readiness Rubric (Appendix B.26) to access the group's readiness and to determine appropriate actions for change.

HISTORY
1. What past or current change efforts can you recall?
2. What did you think about each?
3. How comfortable are you with change in general?

NEED FOR CHANGE
1. Is there a need for improvement in your schools?
2. What are you most dissatisfied with?
3. What changes would you like to see?

WILLINGNESS TO CHANGE
1. Would your group be willing to make changes in the way you do business to accomplish the change needed?
2. Could you give some examples of changes you would be willing to make?
3. Would you make these changes even if you were likely to experience a period of difficulty or were uncomfortable for a period of time?
4. Would these changes be temporary or permanent?
5. Do you think other stakeholders would be willing to make changes even if the changes were difficult and would make them uncomfortable at first?

FAITH IN LEADERSHIP
1. Do you think the current leadership has the ability to successfully accomplish the proposed change? Why or why not?

CHANGE PLAN
1. Do you think the plan that has been described has the potential to achieve the goal(s)? Why or why not?
2. What do you think are the strong points of the plan? The weaknesses?
3. What would you change in the plan to improve it?

SKILLS NECESSARY TO IMPLEMENT
1. Do you think your group has the knowledge/skills necessary to implement the change plan?
2. If not, do you think your group would be willing to acquire the necessary knowledge/skills?
3. How long do you think that would take?
4. Do you think there are some members of your group who, even if willing, would be unable to acquire the necessary knowledge/skills?

From P. Hall, D. Childs-Bowen, A. Cunningham-Morris, P. Pajardo, & A. Simeral, *The Principal Influence: A Framework for Developing Leadership Capacity in Principals* (Alexandria, VA: ASCD, 2016). © 2016 ASCD. Adapted and reprinted from p. 157 of D. Reeves, *Leading Change in Your School* (Alexandria, VA: ASCD, 2009).

APPENDIX B.30: EQUITY LEADERSHIP REFLECTION RUBRIC

DIRECTIONS: Review the rubric descriptions. Reflect on each knowledge, action or skill listed in the chart. As you reflect, determine and record your equity leadership level based on the rubric. For those areas where you are not consciously skilled, think about, commit to, and list the next steps you will take to move to that level. For those areas where you are consciously skilled, think about, commit to, and list the next steps you will take to support identified staff members in moving to the consciously skilled level.

MY LEADERSHIP LEVEL THROUGH AN EQUITY LENS	DESCRIPTION
Level I Unconsciously Unskilled (I don't know what I don't know)	I haven't thought of this. I haven't attempted this in my leadership role. I haven't developed a schema of how this would look at my school.
Level II Consciously Unskilled (I kind of know what I don't know)	I think about this sometimes and know I should do it to support my leadership role. I need to get better at doing this and understand when and how to do it with purpose.
Level III Unconsciously Skilled (I don't know when to use what I know)	I am aware of the significance of this and the impact on my leadership role. I don't know when to use this to maximize my growth as a leader or why this is effective with some staff and not others when I do use it.
Level IV Consciously Skilled (I know what I know and when to use it)	This is always on my mind. I have a purposeful understanding of how it influences my leadership role. I know how I should do this, when to do it, and how to modify it to address the needs of my staff.

KNOWLEDGE, ACTIONS, SKILLS	MY EQUITY LEADERSHIP LEVEL	MY NEXT STEPS
Understands how mindset about race, culture, and language can impact adult interactions with and expectations of their students		
Understands how and why adult mediocrity influences student achievement and performance gaps		
Integrates race, culture, language and equity issues into all instructional leadership actions		
Addresses equity issues involving race, culture, and language as an aspect of staff observation and feedback		

Continued

APPENDIX B.30: EQUITY LEADERSHIP REFLECTION RUBRIC (CONTINUED)

KNOWLEDGE, ACTIONS, SKILLS	MY EQUITY LEADERSHIP LEVEL	MY NEXT STEPS
Challenges and stops questionable school practices that disproportionately impact students of specific ethnic or cultural backgrounds		
Disaggregates student formative and summative assessment results by teacher/course/grade levels and student race/ethnicity for discussions and actions related to instructional practices, student engagement practices, and practices for connecting with students		
Integrates student voice into solving achievement and performance gap issues by eliciting their perceptions of their learning experiences and the school/classroom climate		
Empowers the voice of parents, guardians, and families by eliciting their perceptions on school-related, and achievement-related concerns, and involving them in solutions		

From P. Hall, D. Childs-Bowen, A. Cunningham-Morris, P. Pajardo, & A. Simeral, *The Principal Influence: A Framework for Developing Leadership Capacity in Principals* (Alexandria, VA: ASCD, 2016). © 2016 ASCD. Adapted and used with permission from pp. 28 & 43 of E. Javius, (2005). *Courageous Equity Leadership Toolkit;* available at http://www.edequity.com.

APPENDIX B.31: WHO AM I? STUDENT SELF-ASSESSMENT

DIRECTIONS: Ask students to rate themselves on a scale from 1 to 5 for a variety of classroom and life skills and color in the boxes on the chart to make a bar graph. (Alternately, you can provide descriptors for various levels such as 1="I've never even heard of this"; 2="I can sort of do this"; 3="I can do this"; 4="This is easy for me"; and 5="I'm an expert at this.") See below for a list of suggested skills from which you can choose according to the grade level and backgrounds of your students. Be sure that you include some skills that are not traditional school skills. The point of the exercise is to have students notice that they have both strengths and weaknesses and for you to make connections with your students that will help you get to know them. If you include only school subjects, some students will rate themselves low or high across the board and miss this important message. Consider leaving one or more attribute boxes empty, and ask students to fill in other skills that they would like to rate themselves on. Some skills you could use for this activity are:

Adding in your head
Adding on paper
Asking questions in class
Brainstorming ideas
Building a snowman
Caring for animals
Cleaning up your area
Conducting experiments
Cooking
Dancing
Dividing
Diving
Drawing
Drawing comics
Driving a car
Eating healthy
Exercising
Fixing something that is broken
Following directions
Gardening

Giving directions
Graphing
Hiking
Hitting a baseball
Ice skating
Kayaking
Keeping a diary
Keeping up with current events
Keeping your room neat
Listening to directions
Making a speech
Making change
Making friends
Making up stories
Miniature golf
Multiplying
Painting
Playing an instrument
Playing sports (list:_____)
PowerPoint

Reading
Reading a map
Riding a bike
Rotating objects in your head
Running
Singing
Skateboarding
Snow skiing
Speaking a foreign language
Subtracting
Talking in front of a group
Talking to teachers
Telling jokes
Turning in homework on time
Walking a balance beam
Water skiing
Working alone
Working in a group
Writing poems
Writing stories

Continued

APPENDIX B.31: WHO AM I? STUDENT SELF-ASSESSMENT (CONTINUED)

5									
4									
3									
2									
1									
Skills:									

Once students have completed their graphs, post them around the room and talk about the many ways this information can support how you work together in your classroom.

From P. Hall, D. Childs-Bowen, A. Cunningham-Morris, P. Pajardo, & A. Simeral, *The Principal Influence: A Framework for Developing Leadership Capacity in Principals* (Alexandria, VA: ASCD, 2016). © 2016 ASCD. Adapted and reprinted from p. 50 of C. Strickland, *Tools for High Quality Differentiated Instruction: An ASCD Action Tool* (Alexandria, VA: ASCD, 2007).

APPENDIX B.32: MY STUDENT MATRIX

DIRECTIONS: Use the chart below to get to know your students, acknowledge their strengths, and appreciate their uniqueness.

MY STUDENTS	LIST SOMETHING UNIQUE	LIST A SPECIAL INTEREST, TALENT, OR SKILL	LIST SOMETHING A STUDENT HAS IN COMMON WITH OTHERS

APPENDIX B.33: ETHICAL LEADERSHIP ACTION STEPS GUIDE

PURPOSE: Principal supervisors, coaches, and mentors can integrate the use of the ethics action step guidelines as they provide job-embedded coaching to their principals. The use of the action step guidelines will assure that ethical practices are addressed naturally, as the circumstances occur in coaching experiences.

DIRECTIONS: Use the action steps below to reflect on how the principal being coached or mentored reacts to ethical dilemmas. List next steps you will take as a coach or mentor to support the principal in refining how he or she anticipates and reacts to problems that include ethical dilemmas.

STEP 1: The principal recognizes when there is a possible ethical dilemma that may need attention.
My Next Steps as a Coach/Mentor:

STEP 2: The principal defines the ethical issues involved in an event or problem.
My Next Steps as a Coach/Mentor:.

STEP 3: The principal takes personal responsibility for generating an ethical solution.
My Next Steps as a Coach/Mentor:

STEP 4: The principal figures out what abstract ethical rule(s) might apply to the problem.
My Next Steps as a Coach/Mentor:

STEP 5: The principal suggests a concrete solution using abstract ethical rules that are related to the problem.
My Next Steps as a Coach/Mentor:

STEP 6: The principal prepares for possible repercussions of having acted in what would be considered as an ethical manner.
My Next Steps as a Coach/Mentor:

STEP 7: The principal enacts the ethical solution and reacts appropriately to any stakeholders who may not have agreed with the solution by sharing the ethical reasons for the solution.
My Next Steps as a Coach/Mentor:

From P. Hall, D. Childs-Bowen, A. Cunningham-Morris, P. Pajardo, & A. Simeral, *The Principal Influence: A Framework for Developing Leadership Capacity in Principals* (Alexandria, VA: ASCD, 2016). © 2016 ASCD. Adapted from R. Sternberg,(2011). "Ethics: From Thought to Action". *Educational Leadership* 68(6), 34–39.

APPENDIX B.34: EQUITY AUDIT

DIRECTIONS: Use your demographic information and your responses to the questions below to honestly assess equitable practices in your school or district. Use the results to help principals and schools focus on and create plans to address equitable practices.

STEP 1:

A. Complete the student demographic information for your school or district.

B. Total student enrollment:

C. Ethnicity (note number and percent of each race/ethnicity):

D. Gender (note number and percent of male/female):

E. Free or reduced meals (note number and percent of total population; note number and percent by gender as well as race/ethnicity):

F. Students with disabilities (note number and percent of total population; note number and percent by gender as well as race/ethnicity):

G. Students with limited English proficiency (note number and percent of total population; note number and percent by gender as well as race/ethnicity)

STEP 2: Analyze the context and performance of student groups within your school or district.

1. What is the performance of student groups on state assessments?

2. Which student groups are over- (and under-) represented in special education?

3. Which student groups are over- (and under-) represented in advanced academics/placement?

4. Which student groups are over- (and under-) represented in discipline matters?

5. Which student groups are taught by beginning/novice/rookie teachers?

6. Which courses are taught by beginning/novice/rookie teachers?

Continued

APPENDIX B.34: EQUITY AUDIT (CONTINUED)

STEP 3: Using the responses from the questions in Step 2, consider how much effort will it take to significantly change the current status of each question that will result in more equitable representation?

1. a. very little   b. some   c. a lot   d. overwhelming

2. a. very little   b. some   c. a lot   d. overwhelming

3. a. very little   b. some   c. a lot   d. overwhelming

4. a. very little   b. some   c. a lot   d. overwhelming

5. a. very little   b. some   c. a lot   d. overwhelming

6. a. very little   b. some   c. a lot   d. overwhelming

STEP 4: As a team, create an action plan that addresses the equity practices in your school or district. Determine if you will start with a quick win (choosing an area that would take "very little" effort) or if you will confront a significant area of equity need (selecting an area that might require "overwhelming" effort).

From P. Hall, D. Childs-Bowen, A. Cunningham-Morris, P. Pajardo, & A. Simeral, *The Principal Influence: A Framework for Developing Leadership Capacity in Principals* (Alexandria, VA: ASCD, 2016). © 2016 ASCD.

APPENDIX B.35: LESSON STUDY PROTOCOL

DIRECTIONS: Lesson Study team members can use these steps and the guiding questions provided to plan a lesson study experience, helping teams to analyze the effectiveness of a given lesson, structure, or instructional technique.

STEP 1:   **Determine Lesson Focus.**

1. What content-specific goals and topic will be the focus of the lesson?

   ```
   
   
   ```

2. Which student learning objectives and curricular standards are aligned to the goals/topic?

   ```
   
   
   ```

3. How will information about student understanding of the goal/topic be gathered?

   ```
   
   
   ```

STEP 2:   **Develop Lesson.**

4. What lesson design steps and resources will be used?

   ```
   
   
   ```

5. What are the anticipated student misconceptions, and how will the misconceptions be clarified?

   ```
   
   
   ```

6. Which instructional practices will be implemented for the lesson?

   ```
   
   
   ```

7. How will the detailed lesson plan be shared with the team?

   ```
   
   
   ```

8. Will the lesson be recorded or observed "live"? What protocols will be in place for the lesson observation?

   ```
   
   
   ```

Continued

APPENDIX B.35: LESSON STUDY PROTOCOL (CONTINUED)

STEP 3:   **Engage in Lesson Observation and Reflection.**

9. What guiding questions will be used to identify student look-fors?

10. What guiding questions will be used to encourage lesson study team members' reflection on student learning evidence?

11. What guiding questions will be used to encourage lesson study team member reflection on student engagement evidence?

12. What guiding questions will be used to determine if the lesson goals were met?

13. What guiding questions will be used to plan next steps for lesson study team members?

APPENDIX B.36: REFLECTIVE CYCLE GOALS CHART

DIRECTIONS: Teachers at each stage of the Continuum of Self-Reflection can focus on certain components of the Reflective Cycle to strengthen their growth as reflective practitioners. Use the chart below to select focus areas for goal setting for teachers and those who support, coach, and supervise them.

REFLECTIVE CYCLE GOALS ↓	UNAWARE STAGE	CONSCIOUS STAGE	ACTION STAGE	REFINEMENT STAGE
BUILD AWARENESS	Observe	Note cause/effect relationships	Zoom in on the details	Bring all the variables together
ACT INTENTIONALLY	Think intentionally	Plan with intentionality	Strategize	Move beyond strategy to design
ASSESS IMPACT	Notice learning	Recognize the results of your actions	Consider student thinking as you assess	Assess with a purpose
RESPOND ACCORDINGLY	Make changes	Respond to the needs you see	Respond in the moment	Trust your intuition
REFLECT FREQUENTLY	Practice reflection	Commit to reflecting each day	Develop a pattern of reflection	Cultivate reflexive reflection

From P. Hall, D. Childs-Bowen, A. Cunningham-Morris, P. Pajardo, & A. Simeral, *The Principal Influence: A Framework for Developing Leadership Capacity in Principals* (Alexandria, VA: ASCD, 2016). © 2016 ASCD. Adapted and reprinted from p. 158 of P. Hall, & A. Simeral, *Teach, Reflect, Learn: Building Your Capacity for Success in the Classroom* (Alexandria, VA: ASCD, 2015).

APPENDIX B.37: DEVELOPING SCHOOL-BASED PD PLANS USING THE SIX CS

DIRECTIONS: As you design your school-based professional learning, periodically assess how well you are including the components of the six *Cs* for effective professional development. The following checklist can help guide your thinking and provide discussion points about the components of the six *Cs* for your planning team:

Connected...

☐ Flows from and contributes to the district and building student achievement goals.

☐ Directly relates to student learning and achievement.

☐ Clearly demonstrates how past initiatives can be integrated with new content.

☐ Affects classroom instruction by changing teaching practices.

☐ Matches needs established in analyzing data about student learning and achievement.

Collaborative...

☐ Provides time for teachers to work together to plan for implementation of learning.

☐ Provides venues for participants to share ideas and solve problems.

☐ Establishes procedures and tools for reporting results of collaboration efforts.

☐ Evaluates the collegial environment.

☐ Expects teachers and administrators to work together.

☐ Brings parents and families into the knowledge base and includes them in implementation.

☐ Provides coaching opportunities for participants as they try new ideas and strategies.

Customized...

☐ Includes provisions for meeting different learning needs of participants.

☐ Relates specifically to various content-area applications.

☐ Addresses specific needs of the district and building.

☐ Provides alternatives and options for professional learning.

☐ Builds commitment of individuals.

Coordinated...

☐ Clearly demonstrates alignment with the curriculum.

☐ Provides assistance in integrating past and present initiatives.

☐ Provides for implementation strategies for transitioning between grade-level spans.

☐ Includes classroom-based applications of the PD content.

Continued

APPENDIX B.37: DEVELOPING SCHOOL-BASED PD PLANS USING THE SIX CS (CONTINUED)

Comprehensive...

☐ Includes components of theory, demonstration, practice, and collaboration.

☐ Projects into the future by planning for implementation over a three-to-five-year span.

☐ Includes provisions for bringing new staff members up-to-date.

☐ Provides time lines for delivering and implementing the initiative.

☐ Evaluates implementation efforts and effects on student learning.

Consistent...

☐ Provides a research base to support the PD initiative.

☐ Measures fidelity of implementation efforts.

☐ Spreads learning opportunities at appropriate intervals throughout the year.

☐ Examines how PD initiatives are compatible with participants' beliefs about education.

APPENDIX B.38: ASSESSING PRIOR KNOWLEDGE AND LEARNING PREFERENCES

DIRECTIONS: Those participating in professional development should complete this form prior to beginning professional learning experiences for an identified practice or content area. The information provided will assist the PD planners in differentiating the professional learning in order to meet the needs of those participating.

Identified Practice or Content: _____

How do you view your current knowledge of and experience with this topic? (Check all that apply)

- ☐ Don't know anything about it
- ☐ Have read a little about it
- ☐ Have attended a workshop on it
- ☐ Have read a lot about it
- ☐ Have a grasp of the basic principles underlying it
- ☐ Am acquainted with some strategies related to the topic
- ☐ Sometimes use one or more strategies related to the topic
- ☐ Frequently use strategies related to the topic in my classroom
- ☐ Could deliver this content to others in my building or district

What would you like to learn about the topic? What questions do you have about it?

How do you prefer to learn? (Check all that apply)

- ☐ Through large-group activity
- ☐ Through small-group activity
- ☐ With a partner
- ☐ Independently
- ☐ Other: _____

Continued

APPENDIX B.38: ASSESSING PRIOR KNOWLEDGE AND LEARNING PREFERENCES (CONTINUED)

How do you prefer to share what you've learned with colleagues? (Check all that apply)

☐ Through a presentation to a large group

☐ Through a presentation to a small group

☐ By learning together within a PLC team

☐ By talking with a partner

☐ Through writing

☐ By inviting colleagues into my classroom to observe

☐ Through peer coaching

☐ Other: _____

From P. Hall, D. Childs-Bowen, A. Cunningham-Morris, P. Pajardo, & A. Simeral, *The Principal Influence: A Framework for Developing Leadership Capacity in Principals* (Alexandria, VA: ASCD, 2016). © 2016 ASCD. Adapted and reprinted from p. 51 of S. Beers, *Strategies for Designing, Implementing, and Evaluating Professional Development* (Alexandria, VA: ASCD, 2007). Original source: V. Blake, L. Kiernan, M. D'Arcangelo, & S. Chapman, *Literacy Across the Curriculum* (Alexandria, VA: ASCD, 2003).

APPENDIX B.39: EVALUATING PD IMPACT

DIRECTIONS: Begin thinking about how you will evaluate the results of the implementation of professional development by asking questions about what you want to know. Then, identify what information you can gather, how you will gather it, and who will be responsible for gathering and reporting it. Use the chart below to guide your thinking and planning.

QUESTIONS What do we want to know? What do we need to know to assess the results?	INFORMATION NEEDED How will we know when we have adequately answered the question?	METHOD FOR COLLECTING What sources, process, or documentation could we use?	PROCESS FOR REPORTING By whom, to whom, when, and how will we report?

Review what you have included to determine the comprehensiveness of your evaluation. Have you included the most important things you need to assess? Have you developed an efficient process for data collection that will give you the information you need to move forward?

From P. Hall, D. Childs-Bowen, A. Cunningham-Morris, P. Pajardo, & A. Simeral, *The Principal Influence: A Framework for Developing Leadership Capacity in Principals* (Alexandria, VA: ASCD, 2016). © 2016 ASCD. Adapted and reprinted from p. 49 of S. Beers, *Strategies for Designing, Implementing, and Evaluating Professional Development* (Alexandria, VA: ASCD, 2007).

APPENDIX B.40: ASSESSING ORGANIZATIONAL SUPPORT OF PD

PURPOSE: Teachers, administrators, and all of those who participate in professional learning can use this tool to identify the areas where there is adequate organizational support, at the district and school levels, for effective professional development practices. The checklist can be used in an electronic survey format so that results are easily displayed. The results should be shared with district and school leaders so that actions can be taken in areas identified as needing more support.

Identify those areas where there is adequate support for effective professional development at the district and school levels.

☐ Building-level administrators participate in professional development experiences and are familiar with the content of professional development programs.

☐ District-level personnel are aware of PD efforts and overtly support them.

☐ The professional development goals align with the district and building goals.

☐ Professional development efforts are given adequate financial support.

☐ District-level professional development is tied to school efforts, and a clear connection is made between the two.

☐ An atmosphere of risk taking is prevalent, and teachers and administrators are encouraged to try new strategies.

☐ Professional development design includes provisions for adequate follow-up, including support for time for collaboration.

☐ Communication with others outside the school or district is provided to build support for and understanding of the need for professional development.

☐ Adequate professional development time for presenting information, theory, and demonstration opportunities to learn new content is provided.

☐ School leaders provide ongoing support and encouragement for new initiatives.

☐ A culture of experimentation exists in which teachers are rewarded for efforts related to implementing new ideas.

☐ A spirit of cooperation exists between administration and staff regarding the planning, implementation, and evaluation of professional development efforts.

☐ The needs of individual learners are considered in designing and delivering the professional development program.

☐ A process exists for solving professional development implementation problems.

Continued

APPENDIX B.40: ASSESSING ORGANIZATIONAL SUPPORT OF PD (CONTINUED)

☐ The resources needed for successful implementation of the professional development program are considered and addressed during the planning stage.

☐ Clear targets and expectations for implementation are defined and shared.

☐ Input is sought from participants in the planning and evaluation stages of the professional development program, and this input is used in the decision-making process.

☐ Clear guidelines for the PD decision-making process exist and will be used to make decisions regarding the professional development program.

☐ The content of professional development programs is carefully researched and selected to meet needs identified during an analysis of student achievement data.

From P. Hall, D. Childs-Bowen, A. Cunningham-Morris, P. Pajardo, & A. Simeral, *The Principal Influence: A Framework for Developing Leadership Capacity in Principals* (Alexandria, VA: ASCD, 2016). © 2016 ASCD. Adapted and reprinted from p. 113 of S. Beers, *Strategies for Designing, Implementing, and Evaluating Professional Development* (Alexandria, VA: ASCD, 2007).

APPENDIX B.41: TAKING STOCK OF DISTRIBUTED LEADERSHIP

DIRECTIONS: Engaging in personal reflection about opportunities and obstacles to distributing leadership among staff is important for principals to inform their planning. During reflection, use this template to list practices in place that you could build on or enhance to distribute leadership. Also list opportunities for distributed leadership that aren't currently in place and potential obstacles to moving forward along with resources and incentives needed. Once included, choose a trusted colleague with whom to share your reflections and complete the Next-Step Action Planning Guide (below).

Distributed leadership practices and policies in place in my school
Distributed leadership opportunities I can develop
Distributed leadership obstacles I need to remove
Distributed leadership resources and incentives I need

NEXT-STEP ACTION PLANNING GUIDE:

WHAT IS MY GOAL (What would I like to accomplish?)	WHAT ARE THE ACTION STEPS (How will I accomplish it?)	TIMEFRAME (When will I complete the steps?)	SUPPORT (Who will help me?)	METRIC FOR SUCCESS (How will I gauge the effectiveness?)	OTHER NOTES

APPENDIX B.42: PRINCIPAL MENTOR SELECTION TOOL

DIRECTIONS: Use the samples below to develop interview questions and look-fors when selecting principal mentors in your district. Add as many questions/scenarios as you deem necessary to identify the most promising mentors.

Sample Questions for Mentor Selection Process

1. What are the tenets of successful mentoring?

   Look for: foundational knowledge of best practices in mentoring, including roles of partner, advisor, coach

2. Tell about an experience where you felt your mentoring efforts were successful.

   Look for: insight about approach, feedback, support, growth, changes in the protégé's practice

3. Describe the methodology that you will use to develop a coaching/ mentoring plan.

   Look for: assessing needs, ability to create and execute a plan, ongoing communication, monitoring progress

4. How will you measure the impact of your mentoring efforts?

   Look for: identification of meaningful goals and measurable metrics

5. What adjustments will you make when sufficient progress isn't made?

   Look for: referral to coaching/mentoring plan/goals, utilization, and analysis of metrics

6. Imagine that I (the interviewer) am your protégé, and I confide in you that I am having difficulty garnering staff support of an instructional initiative. Engage me in a conversation to simulate how you would approach the mentor-protégé dialogue.

   Look for: questioning/prompting strategies, trust-building approaches, challenges, encouragement

Possible rating scale for responses:

Not Promising		Shows Potential		Highly Promising
1	2	3	4	5

From P. Hall, D. Childs-Bowen, A. Cunningham-Morris, P. Pajardo, & A. Simeral, *The Principal Influence: A Framework for Developing Leadership Capacity in Principals* (Alexandria, VA: ASCD, 2016). © 2016 ASCD.

APPENDIX B.43: THE HUMAN SIDE OF THE PRINCIPALSHIP MATRIX

PURPOSE: Effective principals demonstrate professionalism in all contexts and interactions. This tool identifies six of the more powerful characteristics of interpersonal professionalism necessary for effective school leadership.

DIRECTIONS: Using the indicators below, answer: To what extent does the principal exhibit this indicator? Supervisors, principal coaches, and other school-based administrators can use or modify this to help leaders gauge their current state and to become aware and responsive in exhibiting these important behaviors. The results of this assessment can help guide goal setting and action planning for continued professional growth.

	DOESN'T EXHIBIT	EXHIBITS AT TIMES, AND MAY NEED SUPPORT	EXHIBITS CONSISTENTLY
Listens thoughtfully to other viewpoints and responds constructively to suggestions and criticism			
Is ethical and transparent, uses good judgment, and maintains confidentiality			
Recognizes and celebrates individual and collective successes of staff and students			
Attends to and fosters professional relationships that result in a positive school culture			
Models care and genuine concern for staff and students			
Cultivates trust and demonstrates respect			

APPENDIX B.44: ACTION RESEARCH PLANNING TEMPLATE

DIRECTIONS: Individually, or with a grade-level, content, or leadership team, complete the chart to create, refine, implement, and monitor an Action Research project.

What question drives this work (what challenge are you attempting to address)?

Planning

STRATEGY NAME	CURRENT (PRE-) LEVELS OF PERFOR- MANCE	TARGET DATE FOR COMPLETION	ASSESSMENT TOOL TO BE USED	STRATEGY FOR IMPLE- MENTATION	TOOLS AND/ OR MATERIALS NEEDED
1.					
2.					
3.					

Continued

APPENDIX B.44: ACTION RESEARCH PLANNING TEMPLATE
(CONTINUED)

Data Collection

STRATEGY NAME	RECORD NOTES AND COLLECT DATA ON THE IMPACT
1.	
2.	
3.	

Reflections on the Process

Analyze the impact of each strategy. Which provided the most effective solution?

How will you adapt the strategy (and/or the other strategies) to increase the positive impact?

APPENDIX B.45: REFLECTIONS ON PROFESSIONAL READING

DIRECTIONS: Use the following format for recording and reporting what you or your small group has learned from professional reading. Add your reflections to your personal learning log or share them with colleagues.

Team name: _____

Members: _____

TITLE:	AUTHOR/SOURCE:

Reflections on what we learned

IMPORTANT POINTS TO REMEMBER/"AHA" MOMENTS:	CONNECTIONS TO WHAT WE ALREADY DO:

Future actions based on what we learned

WHAT WE NEED TO KNOW MORE ABOUT OR HAVE QUESTIONS ABOUT:	PERSONAL ACTIONS WE'LL TAKE TO IMPLEMENT WHAT WE LEARNED:

Bibliography

ASCD (2015). The Whole Child approach to education. Available at: http://www.wholechildeducation. org/about.

Aseltine, J., Faryniarz, J., & Rigazio-DiGilio, A. (2006). *Supervision for learning: A performance-based approach to teacher development and school improvement.* Alexandria, VA: ASCD.

Barth, R., Darnell, B., Lipton, L., & Wellman, B. (2006). *Guide for instructional leaders, Guide 1: An ASCD action tool.* Alexandria, VA: ASCD.

Beers, S. (2007). *Strategies for designing, implementing, and evaluating professional development.* Alexandria, VA: ASCD.

Bernhardt, V. (2009). *Data, data everywhere: Bringing all the data together for continuous school improvement.* London: Routledge.

Bland, J., Sherer, D., Guha, R., Woodworth, K., Shields, P., Tiffany-Morales, J., et al. (2011). *The status of the teaching profession 2011.* Sacramento, CA: Center for the Future of Teaching and Learning at WestEd.

Bossidy, L., & Charan, R. (2002). *Execution: The discipline of getting things done.* New York: Crown Business.

Boudett, K., City, E., & Murnane, R. (2005). *Data wise: A step-by-step guide to using assessment results to improve teaching and learning.* Cambridge, MA: Harvard University Press.

Bridges, W. (1991). *Managing transitions: Making the most of change.* New York: Perseus Books.

Brown, J. (2008). *Educating the whole child: An ASCD action tool.* Alexandria, VA: ASCD.

Buckingham, M. (2005). *The one thing you need to know. . . about great managing, great leading, and sustained individual success.* New York: Free Press.

Burkhauser, S., Gates, S., Hamilton, L., & Ikemoto, G. (2012). *First-year principals in urban school districts: How actions and working conditions relate to outcomes.* Santa Monica, CA: RAND Corporation.

Caine, G., & Caine, R. (2010). *Strengthening and enriching your professional learning community: The art of learning together.* Alexandria, VA: ASCD.

Carroll, L. (1865). *Alice's adventures in Wonderland.* Oxford: Christ Church College.

Childress, S., Elmore, R., Grossman, A., & Johnson, S. (2007). *Managing school districts for high performance: Cases in public education leadership.* Cambridge, MA: Harvard Education Press.

Childs-Bowen, D. (2006). If you build teacher leadership, they will come. *The Learning Principal 2*(3): 2.

Childs-Bowen, D. (2007a). Effective schools maximize time, people. *The Learning Principal 2*(6): 2.

Childs-Bowen, D. (2007b). Personal reflection precedes school assessment. *The Learning Principal 2*(7): 2.

Childs-Bowen, D., Moller, G., & Scrivner, J. (2000) Principals: Leaders of leaders. *NASSP Bulletin 84*(616): 27–34.

City, E., Elmore, R., Fiarman, S., & Teitel, L. (2009). *Instructional rounds in education: A network approach to improving teaching and learning.* Cambridge, MA: Harvard Education Press.

Collins, J. (2001). *Good to great: Why some companies make the leap. . . and others don't.* New York: HarperCollins.

Comer, J. (1995). *School power: Implications of an intervention project.* Houston, TX: Free Press.

Costantino, T. (2010). The critical friends group: A strategy for developing intellectual community in doctoral education. *i.e.: inquiry in education: 1*(2), Article 5. Available at: http://digitalcommons.nl.edu/ie/vol1/iss2/5.

Dalkey, N., & Helmer, O. (1963). An experimental application of the Delphi method to the use of experts. *Management Science 9*(3): 458–467.

Danielson, C. (2006). *Teacher leadership that strengthens professional practice.* Alexandria, VA: ASCD.

Danielson, C. (2007). *Enhancing professional practice: A framework for teaching* (2nd ed.). Alexandria, VA: ASCD.

Dean, C., Hubbell, E. R., Pitler, H., & Stone, B. (2012). *Classroom instruction that works: Research-based strategies for increasing student achievement* (2nd ed.). Alexandria, VA: ASCD.

Deming, W. E. (1993). *The new economics for industry, government, and education.* Boston: MIT Press.

Dewey, J. (1910). *How we think.* New York: Heath.

Dewey, J. (1933). *How we think: A restatement of the relation of reflective thinking to the educative process.* New York: Heath.

Drago-Severson, E. (2004). *Becoming adult learners: Principals and practices for effective development.* New York: Teachers College Press.

DuFour, R. (2002). The learning-centered principal. *Educational Leadership 59*(8): 12–15.

DuFour, R. (2004). What is a professional learning community? *Education Leadership 61*(8): 6–11.

DuFour, R., DuFour, R., Eaker, R., & Many, T. (2010). *Learning by doing: A handbook for professional learning communities at work.* Bloomington, IN: Solution Tree.

Dufour, R., & Eaker, R. (1998). *Professional learning communities at work: Best practices for enhancing student achievement.* Bloomington, IN: National Educational Service.

Dweck, C. (2006). *Mindset: The new psychology of success.* New York: Ballantine.

Easton, L. (Ed.). 2008. *Professional learning designs* (2nd ed.). Oxford, OH: National Staff Development Council.

Easton, L. (2009). *Protocols for professional learning.* Alexandria, VA: ASCD.

Fielding, L., Kerr, N., & Rosier, P. (2004). *Delivering on the promise of the 95% reading and math goals.* Kennewick, WA: New Foundation Press.

Finkel, E. (2012). *Principals as instructional leaders.* District Administration, June 2012. Available at: http://www.districtadministration.com/article/principals-instructional-leaders.

Fisher, D., & Frey, N. (2014). *Better learning through structured teaching: A framework for the gradual release of responsibility* (2nd ed.). Alexandria, VA: ASCD.

Freire, P. (1970). *Pedagogy of the oppressed.* New York: Continuum.

Fullan, M. (2001). *Leading in a culture of change.* San Francisco: Jossey-Bass.

Fullan, M. (2008). *The six secrets of change: What the best leaders do to help organization survive and thrive.* San Francisco: Jossey-Bass.

Fullan, M. (2010). *Motion leadership: The skinny on becoming change savvy.* Thousand Oaks, CA: Corwin Press.

Gabriel, J. (2005). *How to thrive as a teacher leader.* Alexandria, VA: ASCD.

Gabriel, J., & Farmer, P. (2009). *How to help your school thrive without breaking the bank.* Alexandria, VA: ASCD.

Gallup. (2012).*The school leader pipeline: Increasing school performance by selecting and developing future leaders.* Washington, DC: Author.

George, B. (2007). *True north: Discover your authentic leadership.* San Francisco: Jossey-Bass.

Glanz, J. (2002). *Finding your leadership style: A guide for educators.* Alexandria, VA: ASCD.

Goodwin, B. (2011). *Simply better: Doing what matters most to change the odds for student success.* Alexandria, VA: ASCD.

Goodwin, B., & Hubbell, E. R. (2013). *The 12 touchstones of good teaching: A checklist for staying focused every day.* Alexandria, VA: ASCD.

Hall, B., Salamone, J., & Standley, S. (2009). Performance management, succession planning, and professional learning communities. *The District Management Journal,* Vol. 2 (Summer 2009). Boston: District Management Council.

Hall, P. (2004). *The first-year principal.* Lanham, MD: Rowman & Littlefield.

Hall, P. (2011). *Lean on! Motivational lessons for school leaders.* Larchmont, NY: Eye on Education.

Hall, P., & Simeral, A. (2008). *Building teachers' capacity for success: A collaborative approach for coaches and school leaders.* Alexandria, VA: ASCD.

Hall, P., & Simeral, A. (2015). *Teach, reflect, learn: Building your capacity for success in the classroom.* Alexandria, VA: ASCD.

Hattie, J. (2009). *Visible learning: A synthesis of over 800 meta-analyses relating to achievement.* New York: Routledge.

Heifetz, R. (1994). *Leadership without easy answers.* Cambridge, MA: Harvard University Press.

Helmer-Hirschberg, O. (1967). *Analysis of the Future: The Delphi Method.* Santa Monica, CA: RAND. Available at: http://www.rand.org/pubs/papers/P3558

Hess, F., & Kelly, A. (2005). Learning to lead? What gets taught in principal preparation programs. Harvard University Program in Education Policy and Governance. Available at: http://www.hks.harvard.edu/pepg/PDF/Papers/Hess_Kelly_Learning_to_Lead_PEPG05.02.pdf

Hoerr, T. (2005). *The art of school leadership.* Alexandria, VA: ASCD.

Hord, S., Rutherford, W., Huling-Austin, L., & Hall, G. (1987). *Taking charge of change.* Alexandria, VA: ASCD.

Hull, J. (2012). *The principal perspective: Full report.* Center for Public Education. Available at: http://www.centerforpubliceducation.org/principal-perspective

Javius, E. (2009). *Courageous Equity Leadership Toolkit.* San Jose, CA: EDEquity. Available at: http://www.edequity.com

Jenkins, L. (2008). *From systems thinking to systemic action: 48 key questions to guide the journey.* Lanham, MD: Rowman & Littlefield.

Jennings, M. (2007). *Leading effective meetings, teams, and work groups in districts and schools.* Alexandria, VA: ASCD.

Joyce, B., & Showers, B. (1982). The coaching of teaching. *Educational Leadership 40*(1): 4–10.

Kafele, B. (2013). *Closing the attitude gap: How to fire up your students to strive for success.* Alexandria, VA: ASCD.

Kohm, B., & Nance, B. (2007). *Principals who learn: Asking the right questions, seeking the best solutions.* Alexandria, VA: ASCD.

Kotter, J. (1996). *Leading change.* Boston: Harvard Business School Press.

Lambert, L. (1998). *Building leadership capacity in schools.* Alexandria, VA: ASCD.

Lambert, L. (2003). *Leadership capacity for lasting school improvement.* Alexandria, VA: ASCD.

Leithwood K., & Seashore-Louis, K. (2011). *Linking leadership to student learning.* San Francisco: Jossey-Bass.

Leithwood, K., Louis, K. S., Anderson, S., & Wahlstrom, K. (2004). *How leadership influences student learning.* New York: Wallace Foundation.

Lezotte, L., & Snyder, K. (2011). *What effective schools do: Re-envisioning the correlates.* Bloomington, IN: Solution Tree Press.

Marzano, R. (2003). *What works in schools: Translating research into action.* Alexandria, VA: ASCD.

Marzano, R., Pickering, C., & Pollock, J. (2001). *Classroom instruction that works: Research-based strategies for increasing student achievement.* Alexandria, VA: ASCD.

Marzano, R., & Waters, T. (2009). *District leadership that works: Striking the right balance.* Bloomington, IN: Solution Tree.

Marzano, R., Waters, T., & McNulty, B. (2005). *School leadership that works: From research to results.* Alexandria, VA: ASCD.

Medina, J. (2008). *Brain rules: 12 principles for surviving and thriving at work, home, and school.* Seattle: Pear Press.

Meek, A., Champion, R., & Dyer, K. (2004). *Guide for instructional leaders, Guide 3: An ASCD action tool.* Alexandria, VA: ASCD.

Moss, C., & Brookhart, S. (2009). *Advancing formative assessment in every classroom: A guide for instructional leaders.* Alexandria, VA: ASCD.

Moss, C., & Brookhart, S. (2015). *Formative classroom walkthroughs: How principals and teachers collaborate to raise student achievement.* Alexandria, VA: ASCD.

Nin, A. (1961). *Seduction of the minotaur.* Chicago: Swallow Press.

Office of Educational Technology (2015). Future ready schools: Empowering educators through professional learning. Available at: www.tech.ed.gov/FutureReady/Professional-Learning

Pajardo, P. (2009). *A case study of a full year, full-time administrative internship program.* (Doctoral dissertation). University of Virginia.

Parrett, W., & Budge, K. (2012). *Turning high-poverty schools into high-performing schools.* Alexandria, VA: ASCD.

Payzant, T. (2011). *Urban school leadership.* San Francisco: Jossey-Bass.

Pink, D. (2009). *Drive: The surprising truth about what motivates us.* New York: Riverhead Books.

Popham, W. (2008). *Transformative assessment.* Alexandria, VA: ASCD.

Porterfield, K., & Carnes, M. (2008). *Why school communication matters: Strategies from PR professionals.* Lanham, MD: Rowman & Littlefield Education.

Pounder, D., & Crow, G. (2005). Sustaining the pipeline of school administrators. *Educational Leadership 62*(8): 56–60.

Price, H. (2008). *Mobilizing the community to help students succeed.* Alexandria, VA: ASCD.

Rath, T. (2007). *StrengthsFinder 2.0.* New York: Gallup Press.

Rath, T., & Conchie, B. (2008). *Strengths based leadership: Great leaders, teams, and why people follow.* New York: Gallup Press.

Reason, C. (2010). *Leading a learning organization: The science of working with others.* Bloomington, IN: Solution Tree.

Reeves, D. (2002). *The daily disciplines of leadership: How to improve student achievement, staff motivation, and personal organization.* San Francisco: Jossey-Bass.

Reeves, D. (2006). *The learning leader: How to focus school improvement for better results.* Alexandria, VA: ASCD.

Reeves, D. (2008). *Reframing teacher leadership to improve your school.* Alexandria, VA: ASCD.

Reeves, D. (2009). *Leading change in your school: How to conquer myths, build commitment, and get results.* Alexandria, VA: ASCD.

Reeves, D. (2010). *Transforming professional development into student results.* Alexandria, VA: ASCD.

Rooney, J. (2000). Survival skills for the new principal. *Educational Leadership 58*(1): 77–78.

Schmoker, M. (2006). *Results now: How we can achieve unprecedented improvements in teaching and learning.* Alexandria, VA: ASCD.

Skrla, L., Bell, K., & Scheurich, J. (2009). *Using equity audits to create equitable and excellent schools.* Thousand Oaks, CA: Corwin.

Snowden, D., & Boone, M. (2007). *A leader's framework for decision making.* Boston: Harvard Business Publishing.

Stiggins, R., Arter, J., Chappuis, J., & Chappuis, S. (2004). *Classroom assessment* for *student learning: Doing it right—using it well.* Portland, OR: ETS Assessment Training Institute.

Strickland, C. (2007). *Tools for high-quality differentiated instruction: An ASCD action tool.* Alexandria, VA: ASCD.

Stronge, J., Richard, H., & Catano, N. (2008). *Qualities of effective principals.* Alexandria, VA: ASCD.

Stronge, R., Xu, X., Leeper, L., & Tonneson, V. (2013). *Principal evaluation: Standards, rubrics, and tools for effective performance.* Alexandria, VA: ASCD.

Tomlinson, C. (2014). *The differentiated classroom: Responding to the needs of all learners* (2nd ed.). Alexandria, VA: ASCD.

United Nations. (1987). 42/187: Report of the World Commission on Environment and Development. Available: http://www.un.org/documents/ga/res/42/ares42-187.htm

Van Clay, M., Soldwedel, P., & Many, T. (2011). *Aligning school districts as PLCs.* Bloomington, IN: Solution Tree.

Venables, D. R. (2014). *How teachers can turn data into action.* Alexandria, VA: ASCD.

Wiggins, G. (1998). *Educative assessment: Designing assessments to inform and improve student performance.* San Francisco: Jossey-Bass.

Wiggins, G., Brown, J., & O'Connor, K. (2003). *Guide for instructional leaders, Guide 2: An ASCD action tool.* Alexandria, VA: ASCD.

Wiggins, G., & McTighe, J. (2005). *Understanding by design* (2nd ed.). Alexandria, VA: ASCD.

Wooden, J., & Jamison, S. (2004). *My personal best: Life lessons from an all-American journey.* New York: McGraw-Hill.

Zmuda, A., Kuklis, R., & Kline, E. (2004). *Transforming schools: Creating a culture of continuous improvement.* Alexandria, VA: ASCD.

Index

About the Authors

 Veteran school administrator and leadership expert **Pete Hall** has dedicated his career to supporting the improvement of our education systems. In addition to his teaching experiences in Massachusetts, California, and Nevada, he served as a school principal for 12 years in Nevada and Washington. This is his sixth book to accompany over a dozen articles on school leadership. When he's not competing in triathlons, Pete currently works as an educational consultant as a member of the ASCD Faculty and trains educators worldwide. You can contact him via e-mail at Pete.Hall.Faculty@ascd.org or connect on Twitter at @EducationHall.

 **Deborah Childs-Bowen** is an internationally recognized transformational educator having served in diverse roles as teacher, principal, district administrator, educational researcher, and university professor. She was past president of Learning Forward (NSDC) and a Marzano consultant. Her knowledge, expert facilitation, executive coaching, and school improvement practices enhance transferring research into application. Deborah is a contributing author to books, toolkits, and professional journals through SERVE, ASCD, NSDC, Corwin, and NASSP. She is chief learning officer with Creative Mind Enterprise, building capacity and equitable learning opportunities that improve practice for educators and learning for all students. She can be reached at deborah@creativemindenterprise.com.

Ann Cunningham-Morris has served educators for over 35 years. She is the former director of professional development for ASCD. She has also been a district-level instructional administrator, school-based administrator, teacher leader, and classroom teacher in seven different states. Additionally, Ms. Cunningham-Morris is an ASCD Faculty member and has served as an educational consultant to many school systems throughout the world in the areas of leadership development, curriculum development, effective professional learning, and instructional best practices. She has written articles, blogs, and provided interviews on these topics for professional publications. She can be reached at acunning.faculty@ascd.org or on Twitter at @ancmo

Phyllis Pajardo is presently the assistant superintendent in Fairfax City, VA, schools. Prior to that, Phyllis served Fairfax County (Virginia) Public Schools for 34 years; she was the assistant superintendent of Human Resources as well as Cluster II, where she was "lead learner" for 28 schools/principals. Phyllis has been an elementary teacher, consulting teacher, assistant principal, principal, specialist, project manager, and director. She is an adjunct faculty for George Mason University and the University of Virginia and serves on the ASCD Faculty, facilitating professional learning on leadership and consulting on leadership development approaches. A native Virginian, Phyllis's dissertation was published in 2009. She loves mentoring and developing aspiring leaders, watching professional basketball and football, listening to contemporary jazz and gospel music, and traveling with her family.

Veteran educator **Alisa Simeral** has guided school-based reform efforts as a teacher, dean, instructional coach, and professional developer. Her emphasis is, and always has been, improving the adult-input factors that contribute to increased student-output results. She has spent the past 10 years studying and writing on this topic, and she is the coauthor of several ASCD books. Alisa currently works as both a district-level instructional coach in Reno, Nevada, and educational consultant on the ASCD Faculty. Her mantra is "When our teachers succeed, our students succeed." You can contact her via email at Alisa.Simeral.Faculty@ascd.org or catch her Twitter feed at @AlisaSimeral.

Related ASCD Resources

At the time of publication, the following ASCD resources were available (ASCD stock numbers appear in parentheses). For up-to-date information about ASCD resources, go to www.ascd.org. You can search the complete archives of *Educational Leadership* at http://www.ascd.org/el.

ASCD Edge®
Exchange ideas and connect with other educators on the social networking site ASCD Edge at http://ascdedge.ascd.org/

Print Products
Balanced Leadership for Powerful Learning: Tools for Achieving Success In Your School by Bryan Goodwin, Greg Cameron, and Heather Hein (#112025)

Building Teachers' Capacity for Success: A Collaborative Approach for Coaches and School Leaders by Pete Hall and Alisa Simeral (#109002)

Improving Student Learning One Principal At a Time by Jane E. Pollock and Sharon m. Ford (#109006)

Learning From Lincoln: Leadership Practices for School Success by Harvey Alvy and Pam Robbins (#110036)

Never Underestimate Your Teachers: Instructional Leadership for Excellence in Every Classroom by Robyn R. Jackson (#110028)

The Principal 50: Critical Leadership Questions for Inspiring Schoolwide Excellence by Baruti K. Kafele (#115050)

Qualities of Effective Principals by James H. Stronge, Holly B. Richard, and Nancy Catano (#108003)

Teach, Reflect, Learn: Building Your Capacity for Success by Pete Hall and Alisa Simeral (#115040)

THE WHOLE CHILD The Whole Child Initiative helps schools and communities create learning environments that allow students to be healthy, safe, engaged, supported, and challenged. To learn more about other books and resources that relate to the whole child, visit www.wholechildeducation.org.

For more information: send e-mail to member@ascd.org; call 1-800-933-2723 or 703-578-9600, press 2; send a fax to 703-575-5400; or write to Information Services, ASCD, 1703 N. Beauregard St., Alexandria, VA 22311-1714 USA.